A Turning of Keys

Poets and Norfolk

1460~1991

Peter J. Beer

Larks Press

Published at the Larks Press
Ordnance Farmhouse, Guist Bottom
Dereham NR20 5PF
Tel/Fax 01328 829207

Printed by the Lanceni Press
Garrood Drive, Fakenham

September 2003

To Andrew, at whose family house
time was unregulated

British Library Cataloguing-in-Publication Data
A catalogue record for this book is available
from the British Library

ISBN 1 904006 14 0

PREFACE

The collective legacy of poets who have shared a connection with the county of Norfolk is one largely unsung. The book is born of this casual realisation.

A quickening curiosity was soon suggesting fresh, and sometimes unexpected, perspectives upon the lives of familiar names: Swinburne's passion for sea-bathing, for instance, or the solitary schoolboy expeditions of W.H. Auden, seemed to be hinting at truths at the heart of their poetic natures. And in the lives of the lesser-known poets – whose reputations have long declined towards obscurity – there began to re-emerge aspects of humanity worthy of something better than their accumulated neglect.

All but three of the poets lived part of their lives – in R.H. Mottram's case, almost his entire life – beneath the fickle Norfolk skies that readers will no doubt hold in common and sometimes exasperated affection. Few, if any, of them inhabited a watered garden; rather they wrote their poetry out of the stony ground of their human fallibility. A shared vulnerability alone is offered as justification for the book. The reader must decide how much light has filtered through doorways now that the keys have been turned.

For kind permissions and use of copyright materials my grateful acknowledgements are due to the Brotherton Library of the University of Leeds; Christ Church Library, Oxford; the Court of the Company of Watermen and Lightermen of the River Thames; Norfolk Museums and Archaeology Service; British Museum; Faber and Faber Ltd for permission to reproduce items of juvenilia, 'Loneliness' and lines from 'Letter to Lord Byron' from the *Collected Poems* of W.H. Auden and 'At Thurgarton Church' and 'Morning in Norfolk' from the *Collected Poems* of George Barker; Norfolk Heritage Centre; Norwich Castle Museum and Art Gallery; A.P. Watt Ltd on behalf of Mrs A.S. Hankinson for permission to reproduce 'Afternoon Tea', 'Up the Line' and 'The Deserted Church Tower on Sidestrand Cliff' from R.H. Mottram's collection, *Poems New and Old;* and the Provost and Fellows of Worcester College, Oxford.

My warmest personal thanks are due to Christopher Bromley-Martin who read the book in typescript. Without his invaluable suggestions and guidance the book would be the poorer. My gratitude goes to Peter Virgin for his further encouragement and constructive criticism; to Keith and the Reverend Angela Dugdale, Sophia Hankinson, John Neill, Margaret Sharman, Olga Ward, Nicholas Warns and Dr Clive Wilkins-Jones who assisted my researches in various ways. I should like to thank the staff of the University of East Anglia Library for so efficiently procuring books for me, some through the British Library service. Finally, I owe a special debt of gratitude to Susan Yaxley (of the Larks Press) whose patience and encouragement have not wavered.

Peter J. Beer

CONTENTS

ILLUSTRATIONS

John Skelton

John Skelton ?1460-1529

Parishioners were vexed that John Skelton, while Rector of Diss, should keep a mistress. And this was no casual concubinage, for there were a number of children. A contemporary biographer, Braynewode, further claimed, though in error, that on his deathbed the poet confessed to having married her in secret.

When complaints were made to the worldly Bishop Nikke of Norwich, Skelton attempted to repair a damaged reputation with a gift of two capons for his supper. He was at first rebuffed, yet remained unchastened.

> 'If your lordship knew the names of these [capons], ye would be content to take them.'
> 'Why, caitiff?' quod the bishop hastily and angerly, 'what be their names?'
> 'I wis, my lord,' quod Skelton, 'this [capon] is called Alpha, [that] is *primus*, the first, and this is called O[mega], that is *nouissimus*, the last. And for the more plain understanding of my mind, if it please your lordship to take them, I promise you this Alpha is the first that ever I gave you, and this O[mega] is the last that ever I will give you while I live!'[1]

The following Sunday he turned his attention to the complainants he knew to be 'worse than knaves.' He dangled from the pulpit his naked child for all the parish to see, upbraiding them in thoroughly Skeltonian fashion for bringing a complaint out of mere jealousy.

> 'You have foul wives, and I have a fair wench – of the which I have begotten a fair boy...Is not this child as fair as is the best of all yours? It is not like a pig, nor a calf...If I had,' said Skelton, 'brought forth this child without arms or legs, or that it was deformed, being a monstrous thing, I would never have blamed you to have complained to the bishop of me. But to complain without cause!'[2]

In their retelling, Skelton's 'merry conceits' were often distorted, and some were of doubtful attribution. There is record, for example, of his refusing a friar use of the pulpit for the purpose of promulgating a papal bull, an act which would have been inconsistent with his known loyalty to the traditions of pre-Reformation faith. Yet he evidently relishes his opportunity with all the fervour of a Protestant propagandist: 'A bull begets a calf,' he is said to have railed, 'but here, contrary to nature, a calf hath gotten a bull; for this friar, being a calf, hath gotten a bull of the Bishop of Rome.'[3]

This Norfolk rector was more than a mere scandalous cleric. His appointment as 'Poet Laureate' was confirmed by the universities of Cambridge, Oxford and Louvain.[4] Moreover, he ranked among the men of high intellect engaged by Henry VII's mother, the formidable Lady Margaret Beaufort, to tutor her grandson, the future Henry VIII.

Skelton's brief was to guide the prince's rudimentary education. 'The honour of England I learned to spell,' he acknowledged; and he wrote for the prince's edification a handbook of earnest maxims, *Speculum Principis*, in which (with a fine irony) the boy was advised to 'pick out a wife for himself and love her alone.'[5]

The tutoring ended when Henry (aged eleven) became Prince of Wales on the death from consumption of his elder brother, Arthur. Skelton then left the moated retreat at Eltham, in Kent, which had been Henry's home for most of his childhood, but remained at court until his appointment to Diss (in c.1503).

In his choice of verse form, Skelton is often happy to abandon the polished conventions of mediaeval court poetry in favour of a playful unorthodoxy:

> For though my rhyme be ragged,
> Tattered and jagged,
> Rudely rain-beaten,
> Rusty and moth-eaten,
> If ye take well therewith,
> It hath in it some pith.
> (Colin Clout ll.53-58)

In the Diss poems 'Ware the Hawk' and 'Philip Sparrow' the characteristics known as 'Skeltonics' are fully developed. In short lines, with irregular beats, the accents are freely placed as if sounding an echo of the plain chant familiar to Skelton in the liturgy of the Church. Alliteration and repetition abound, and we find Skelton's fondness for rhyme which elsewhere in his work becomes more of a distraction.

Ware the Hawk

One St John's Eve, a 'lewd' neighbouring curate chose to train a pair of hawks within the Rector's church of St Mary the Virgin. When Skelton arrived – to find the doors bolted against interruption – he entered his church by a secret way. The tower incorporates an archway through which processions may pass round the precincts. By using a small door to the narrow staircase within the archway's outer wall, he gained alternative access to the tower from which (in Skelton's time) it was possible to descend into the nave.

That this was the feast of John the Baptist's beheading, served only to deepen a sense of outrage. A day that recalls a violent death on the orders of Herod, and a prefiguring of the Passion of Christ, ends for Skelton with the blood of a pigeon upon the altar, and hawk's dung upon the corporal (the communion cloth).[6] Yet he could not resist the play of irony: the profanity, he says, took place *'Tempore vesperatum,/ Sed non secundum Sarum'* (at the time of vespers, but not according to the Sarum use).

Skelton takes for his title the cry of a falconer urging his hawk to make a kill.

> ...I shall make relation,
> By way of apostrophation,
> Under supportation
> Of your patient toleration,
> How I, Skelton Laureate,
> Devisèd and also wrate
> Upon a lewd curàte,
> A parson beneficèd,
> But nothing well advisèd.
> He shall be as now nameless,
> But he shall not be blameless,
> Nor he shall not be shameless;
> For sure he wrought amiss
> To hawk in my church at Diss.
> This fond frantic falconer,
> With his polluted pawtener

2

As priest unreverent,
Straight to the sacrament
He made his hawk to fly,
With hugeous shout and cry.
The high altar he stripped naked;
Thereon he stood and crakèd;
He shook down all the clothès,
And sware horrible oathès,
Before the face of God,
By Moses and Aaron's rod,
Ere that he hence yede
His hawk should prey and feed
Upon a pigeon's maw.
The blood ran down raw
Upon the altar stone;
The hawk tirèd on a bone;
And in the holy place
She dungèd there a chase
Upon my corporas face...[7]

Observate

His second hawk waxèd gery,
And was with flying weary;
She had flowen so oft,
That on the rood loft
She perchèd her to rest.
The falconer then was prest,
Came running with a dow,
And cried 'Stow, stow, stow!'
But she would not bow.
He then, to be sure,
Callèd her with a lure.
Her meat was very crude,
She had not well endued;
She was not clean ensaimèd,[8]
She was not well reclaimèd:
But the falconer unfainèd
Was much more feebler brainèd.
The hawk had no list
To come to his fist;
She lookèd as she had the frounce;
With that he gave her a bounce
Full upon the gorge.
I will not feign nor forge –
That hawkè with that clap
Fell down with evil hap.

3

The church doors were sparrèd,
Fast bolted and barrèd,
Yet with a pretty gin
I fortuned to come in,
This rebel to behold,
Whereof I him controlled.
But he saidè that he would,
Against my mind and will,
In my church hawkè still.

Considerate

...He said he would not let
His houndès for to fet,[9]
To hunt there by liberty
In the despite of me,
And to halloo there the fox.
Down went my offering-box,
Book, bell, and candle,
All that he might handle –
Cross, staff, lectern, and banner,
Fell down in this manner.

Deliberate

...This falconer then 'gan shout,
'These be my gospellers,
These be my epistolers,
These be my choristers
To helpè me to sing,
My hawks to matins ring!'
In this priestly gydìng
His hawk then flew upon
The rood with Mary and John.
Dealt he not like a fon?
Dealt he not like a daw?
Or else is this God's law,
Decrees or decretàls,
Or holy synodals,
Or else provincials,
Thus within the walls
Of holy Church to deal,
Thus to ring a peal,
With his hawkès bells?
Doubtless such losels
Make the church to be
In small authority:
A curate in speciall
To snapper and to fall

Into this open crime!
To look on this were time.

Pensitate

...Ware the hawk!
Apostata Julianus,
Nor yet Nestorianus,
Thou shalt nowhere read
That they did such a deed,
To let their hawkès fly
Ad ostium tabernaculi,
In que est corpus Domine![10]
Cave hoc,
Doctor Dawcock!

Ware the hawk!
Thus doubtless ye ravèd,
Diss church ye thus depravèd;
Wherefore, as I be savèd,
Ye are therefore beknavèd:
Quare? quia Evangelia,
Concha et conchylia,
Accipter et sonalia,
Et bruta animalia,
Caetera quoque talia
Tibi sunt aequalia![11]
Unde hoc,
Domine Dawcock?
Ware the hawk!...

Philip Sparrow

This epitaph for a pet bird, written at the request of a young woman, Jane Scrope, was singled out by C.S. Lewis as 'our first great poem of childhood'. What he had in mind was the poet's success in conveying the childlike play of her emotions. And though the gentle mockery they invite is understandable, Skelton does not compromise the melting tenderness he feels for her. It is an intimate and disarming portrayal.

Before the introduction of the canary, a sparrow was highly prized; it would be housed in a gilt cage and fed the most delicate of morsels.[12]The deep affection Jane reserved for Philip no doubt eased the pain of recent memory. She had, in all probability, witnessed the execution of her stepfather, Sir John Wyndham of Felbrigg, at Tower Hill in May 1520. He had been caught in the web of suspicion that entrapped the relations and friends of the Earl of Suffolk, the prominent Yorkist proclaimed traitor in November 1501.

Accompanied by her mother, Lady Eleanor, Jane found solace within the small community of Benedictine nuns of St Mary's Priory, at Carrow in Norwich. Daily attendance at Mass was the only observance required of her as a lay boarder; she read, or sewed, or idled in desultory contentment.

5

On account of his friendship with Jane's father, the late Sir John Scrope of Bentley in Yorkshire, Skelton would have been a welcome visitor.

'Placebo Domino in regione vivorum' (I shall please the Lord in the land of the living) is the brief antiphon which opens the Office of Vespers of the Dead. Jane's words and thoughts supply the responses, and shape her private meditation:

> *Pla ce bo!*
> Who is there, who?
> *Di le xi!*[13]
>
> Dame Margery.
> *Fa, re, my, my.*
> Wherefore and why, why?
> For the soul of Philip Sparrow
> That was slain at Carrow,
> Among the Nunės Black.
> For that sweet soulės sake,
> And for all sparrows' souls
> Set in our bead-rolls,
> *Pater noster qui,*
> With an *Ave Mari,*
> And with the corner of a Creed,
> The more shall be you meed.
>
> When I remember again
> How my Philip was slain,
> Never half the pain
> Was between you twain,
> Pyramus and Thisbe,
> As then befell to me.
> I wept and I wailèd,
> The teares down hailèd,
> But nothing it availèd
> To call Philip again,
> Whom Gib, our cat, hath slain.
>
> ...Unneth I cast mine eyes
> Toward the cloudy skies.
> But when I did behold
> My sparrow dead and cold,
> No creature but that wold
> Have ruèd upon me,
> To behold and see
> What heaviness did me pang:
> Wherewith my hands I wrang,
> That my sinews cracked,
> As though I had been racked,
> So painèd and so strainèd
> That no life wellnigh remainèd.

6

I sighèd and I sobbed,
For that I was robbed
Of my sparrow's life.
O maiden, widow, and wife,
Of what estate ye be,
Of high or low degree,
Great sorrow then ye might see,
And learn to weep at me!
Such painès did me frete
That mine heart did beat,
My visage pale and dead,
Wan, and blue as lead:
The pangs of hateful death
Wellnigh had stopped my breath.

...It was so pretty a fool,
It would sit on a stool,
And learnèd after my school
For to keep his cut,[14]
With 'Philip, keep your cut!'

It had a velvet cap,
And would sit upon my lap,
And seck after small wormès,
And sometimes white bread-crumbès;
And many times and oft
Between my breastès soft
It wouldè lie and rest;
It was proper and prest.

Sometime he would gasp
When he saw a wasp;
A fly or a gnat,
He would fly at that;
And prettily he would pant
When he saw an ant.
Lord, how he would pry
After the butterfly!
Lord, how he would hop
After the gressop!
And when I said, 'Phip, Phip!'
Then he would leap and skip,
And take me by the lip.
Alas, it will me slo
That Philip is gone me fro!

Si in i qui ta tes...[15]
Alas, I was evil at ease!

7

De pro fun dis cla ma vi,[16]
When I saw my sparrow die!

...I took my sampler once
Of purpose, for the nonce,
To sew with stitches of silk
My sparrow white as milk,
That by representation
Of his image and fashìon
To me it might import
Some pleasure and comfòrt,
For my solace and sport.
But when I was sewing his beak,
Methought my sparrow did speak,
And opened his pretty bill,
Saying, 'Maid, ye are in will
Again me for to kill,
Ye prick me in the head!'
With that my needle waxèd red,
Methought, of Philip's blood;
Mine hair right upstood,
I was in such a fray
My speech was taken away.
I cast down that there was,
And said, 'Alas, alas,
How cometh this to pass?'
My fingers, dead and cold,
Could not my sampler hold:
My needle and thread
I threw away for dread.
The best now that I may
Is for his soul to pray:
A porta inferi[17]...
Good Lord, have mercy
Upon my sparrow's soul,
Written in my bead-roll!...

The birds Jane chooses to take part in Philip's funeral – there are seventy-seven in number – would almost all be known to her as native to East Anglia. They are given moral and symbolical characteristics as in the mediaeval bestiaries.

Lauda, anima mea, Dominum![18]
To weep with me look that ye come
All manner of birdès in your kind;
See none be left behind.
To mourning lookè that ye fall
With dolorous songès funerall,
Some to sing, and some to say,

Every birdé in his lay.
The goldfinch, the wagtail;
The jangling jay to rail,
The fleckèd pie to chatter
Of his dolorous matter;
And robin redbreast,
He shall be the priest
The requiem mass to sing,
Softly warbeling,
With help of the reed sparrow,
And the chatteringè swallow,
This hearsè for to hallow;
The lark with his long toe;
The spink, and the martinet alsò;
The shoveller with his broad beak;
The dotterel, that foolish peke,
And also the mad coot,
With baldè face to toot;
The fieldfare and the snite;
The crow and the kite;
The raven, called Rolfè,
His plain-song to sol-fa;
The partridge, the quail;
The plover with us to wail;
The wood-hack, that singeth 'chur'
Hoarsely, as he had the mur;
The lusty chanting nightingale;
The popinjay to tell her tale,
That toteth oft in a glass,
Shall read the Gospel at mass;
The mavis with her whistle
Shall read there the Epistle.
But with a large and a long
To keep just plain-song,
Our chanters shall be the cuckoo,
The culver, the stockdowe,
With 'peewit' the lapwing,
The Versicles shall sing...

And now the dark cloudy night
Chaseth away Phoebus bright,
Taking his course toward the west,
God send my sparrow's soul good rest!
Requiem aeternam dona eis, Domine! [19]
Fa, fa, fa, mi, re, re,
A por ta in fe ri,
Fa, fa, fa, mi, mi.

Credo videre bona Domini,[20]
I pray God, Philip to heaven fly!
Domine, exaudi orationem meam![21]
To heaven he shall, from heaven he came!
Do mi nus vo bis cum!
Of all good prayers God send him some!
    Oremus,
Deus, cui proprium est misereri et parcere,[22]
On Philip's soul have pity!
For he was a pretty cock,
And came of a gentle stock,
And wrapt in a maiden's smock,
And cherishèd full daintily,
Till cruel fate made him to die:
Alas, for doleful destiny!
But whereto should I
Longer mourn or cry?
To Jupiter I call,
Of heaven imperial,
That Philip may fly
Above the starry sky,
To tread the pretty wren,
That is our Lady's hen.
Amen, amen, amen!

The Commendations

...How shall I report
All the goodly sort
Of her featurès clear,
That hath none earthly peer?
The favour of her face
Ennewèd all with grace,
Comfort, pleasure, and solàce.
My heart doth so enbrace,
And so hath ravished me
Her to behold and see,
That in wordès plain
I cannot me refrain
To look on her again...

The Indy sapphire blue
Her veinès doth ennew;
The orient pearl so clear,
The whiteness of her lere;
Her lusty ruby ruddès
Resemble the rose buddès;
Her lippès soft and merry
Enbloomed like the cherry:

It were a heavenly bliss
Her sugared mouth to kiss.
Her beauty to augment,
Dame Nature hath her lent
A wart upon her cheek, –
Whoso list to seek
In her visàge a scar, –
That seemeth from afar
Like to radiant star,
All with favour fret,
So properly it is set!...

...Her kirtle so goodly lacèd,
And under that is bracèd
Such pleasures that I may
Neither write nor say!
Yet though I write with ink,
No man can let me think,
For thought hath liberty,
Thought is frank and free;
To think a merry thought
It cost me little nor nought.
Would God mine homely style
Were polishèd with the file
Of Cicero's eloquence,
To praise her excellence!...

Skelton ended his residence at Diss in 1512, and returned to a court awake to the capacious ambitions of Thomas Wolsey, the butcher's son from Ipswich, whom he was to mock for his 'greasy genealogy'. In his satires against Wolsey, 'Colin Clout' and the vituperative 'Why Come Ye Not to Court?', the poet, who enjoyed the patronage of the Countess of Surrey, wife of the Duke of Norfolk's son (Thomas Howard), stands with an aristocracy whose rightful place in the counsels of the king had been usurped through the Cardinal's rise to power.[23] Skelton gained respite from the strains of his quarrel when, for short periods (in 1521 and 1522), he was a member of the Countess's household at Sheriff-Hutton, the Howard seat near York. He wrote there the allegorical poem, 'Garland of Laurel', in gratitude for the gift of an embroidered chaplet given by the ladies of the household to honour him as poet.[24] And then the attacks on Wolsey ceased. In the dedications of his final poems, he had even come to regard him as his patron.

Critics have placed Skelton variously 'like a solid rock of conservatism'[25] amid the currents of Renaissance humanism, and as 'the first poet to catch the transitional spirit of his times'.[26] Foremost, he was priest, with a personal, spiritual history. As C.S. Lewis has said: 'He stands out of the streamy historical process, an unmistakable individual, a man we have met.'[27]

11

Henry Howard, Earl of Surrey ?1517-1547

In a portrait which hangs in the Barons' Hall at Arundel Castle, the Earl of Surrey is presented as a standing figure of surpassing nobility. He wears the finest doublet adorned with silver filigree and bears across the chest the chain collar of the Order of the Garter from which depends the jewel of St George (known as the Great George).[1] A pair of Renaissance statues flank the arch which frames him, each resting one arm within architrave scrolls, while the other supports shields of unequivocal pedigree: to the left, the arms of Thomas of Brotherton, Earl of Norfolk and son of Edward I; to the right, those of Thomas of Woodstock, the son of Edward III and in the lineage of Surrey's mother, Elizabeth Stafford. The eye, however, is drawn to Surrey's own right arm resting upon a broken Ionian column, and, as if by invitation, to the abbreviated Latin inscription on the tablet below: SAT SVPER EST – 'It is enough to prevail'. Surrey, who never acquired the political acumen necessary for the protection of Howard interests at Court, succeeds, by means of a portrait 'of emblematic power', in laying claim by right of birth to what his biographer has called 'the continuity of honour'.[2]

Surrey believed that the influence of the rival Seymour faction upon Henry VIII impugned this honour: 'These new men love no nobility',[3] he warned. Certainly, they were consummate opportunists. When, for instance, the first of Henry's Howard Queens, Surrey's cousin Anne Boleyn, was delivered of a dead boy, it was Sir Edward Seymour who at once 'orchestrated' the power of his sister, Jane, by thwarting Anne's attempts to gain access to the King.[4] When Jane became Queen, Seymour was ennobled as Viscount Beauchamp and given a place in the Privy Chamber. A peerage, as Earl of Hertford, soon followed.

A man of 'febrile impatience',[5] Surrey's behaviour towards his enemies increasingly bore the taint of hubris. When, at Hampton Court, Seymour implied that Surrey was not unsympathetic to the cause of the peasant rising of 1537 (known as the Pilgrimage of Grace), Surrey had struck him within the grounds of the palace. He was excused the ritual severing of his right hand, the penalty prescribed for such acts committed when the king was in residence. Instead, in the course of a summer of imprisonment at Windsor, there was time enough for 'a special animosity' to fester.[6] And when the third Duke of Norfolk, Surrey's father, a master of expedient machination, moved to end the rancour by proposing a marriage between his widowed daughter Mary and Hertford's younger brother, Sir Thomas Seymour, Surrey opposed it. It was Mary – earlier married to Henry's bastard son, Henry Fitzroy, Duke of Richmond and Somerset and the close friend of Surrey in their adolescence – who was to bring evidence against him with all the bitterness of sibling treachery.

As was proper to men of the Renaissance, Surrey aspired to noble virtue (as his mediaeval forebears had), through the chivalric quest for personal glory and the praise which flowed from it.[7] With the appearance of Thomas Nashe's romance, *The Unfortunate Traveller* (1594), Surrey's exploits were to become the stuff of legend. To Alexander Pope, writing in 1713, he was close to canonisation:

> Here noble Surrey felt the sacred Rage,
> *Surrey*, the *Granville* of a former age:
> Matchless his pen, victorious was his lance;
> Bold in the lists, and graceful in the Dance:
> (Windsor Castle, ll.291-294)

At a joust held on May Day 1540 in honour of Anne of Cleves, the violence of Surrey's clashes with one of the 'new men', John Dudley, the future Viscount Lisle, won Henry's admiration. Mailed gloves were shattered, yet Surrey was never un-horsed.[8] In warfare he was, by repute, a 'chivalric hawk',[9] effective as a skirmisher in the campaign against Francis I of France, but thought by a nervous Privy Council to favour rash encounters which left him vulnerable to charges of self-interest. In 'an episode of total dishonour',[10] which was the failed attempt in January 1546 upon the fortress of Châtillon, near St Etienne, blame was laid squarely by the Welsh chronicler, Gruffydd, upon Surrey, whom he castigated for his 'pride, arrogance, and empty confidence in his own unreasoning bravery'.[11] Though French losses among the soldiery outnumbered those of the English, the loss of thirteen gentlemen was a disgrace which touched the King's honour. As a direct result, his command was transferred to Hertford. For his services in the field, Surrey acquired the conventual buildings and estates of Wymondham Abbey,[12] but he was never to set foot in France again. The barb he aimed at Hertford was to prove futile: 'My lord of Hertford shall smart for replacing me in France.'[13]

In his thirteenth year Surrey had been installed at Windsor as Richmond's companion, in the hope, as Norfolk put it, of his becoming Richmond's 'preceptor and tutor that he may attain both knowledge and virtue.'[14] It was a male friendship of a kind then pervasive, a bond of intimacy and eager idealism that nurtured Surrey's poetic sensibility and informed their taste for expressions of the Renaissance mind.[15] In 'The Windsor Elegy', Surrey honours the relationship as being one of 'sweet accord' and endows it with the trappings of Arthurian romance. He recalls their youthful 'diverse change of play' – the tests of courage in the tilting-yard, the games of 'nimbleness and strength' and chases of 'the fearful hart'; then, in 'secret groves', the sharing of confidences, 'wanton talk' and telling of 'our ladies' praise'.

For most of the year 1533 they were guests of Francis I at Paris and Fontainebleau, where they relished the literary and aesthetic riches then enjoyed at the French court in the decade before the death of Leonardo da Vinci. They would have heard Italian voices reading Dante and, in the unrhymed verse then fashionable, Surrey found models for his original style in blank verse which, with the English sonnet, is his gift to poetry.[16] In the King's Pavilion of Pomona (at Fontainebleau) were displayed expressions of a new artistic landscape which 'combined ennobling forms of eroticism and idealized art'[17] of a sensuousness unknown in England. And on the walls of the vestibule leading to the baths, whose design bore resemblance to those of ancient Rome, was hung 'the greatest collection of art in northern Europe', where could be seen Leonardo's 'Mona Lisa' and his 'Virgin of the Rocks'.[18]

Three years after their return to Court, Richmond died of consumption. Surrey was utterly forlorn. Richmond bequeathed to him his favourite horse, a black jennet, together with its saddle and harness. Surrey, it seems, considered remembering his friend in the Arundel portrait – on the tablet where finally appeared the motto SAT SVPER EST.

The heroic quatrains of 'The Windsor Elegy', written in memory of Richmond during Surrey's imprisonment for striking Seymour, bear the imprint of other Howard indictments. Anne Boleyn had gone to the scaffold in May 1536 and Surrey's uncle, Lord Thomas Howard, died the next year while imprisoned in the Tower for marrying in secret the King's niece, Lady Margaret Douglas. For Surrey, Windsor had become both 'a metonymy for England',[19] threatened by such loss of noble blood, and a name resonant with a personal grief. Of his elegy, a Victorian critic has written: 'I know of few verses in the whole range of human poetry in which the voice of nature utters the accents of grief with more simplicity and truth; it seems to me to be the most pathetic personal elegy in English poetry.'[20]

The Windsor Elegy

So cruel a prison, how could betide, alas,
As proud Windsor, where I, in lust and joy,
With a king's son my childish years did pass,
In greater feast than Priam's sons of Troy.

Where each sweet place returns a taste full sour.
The large green courts, where we were wont to hove,
With eyes cast up unto the maidens' tower,
And easy sighs, such as folk draw in love.

The stately sales; the ladies bright of hue,
The dances short, long tales of great delight,
With words and looks that tigers could but rue,
Where each of us did plead the other's right.

The palm play, where, despoilèd for the game,
With dazèd eyes oft we by gleams of love
Have missed the ball and got sight of our dame,
To bait her eyes which kept the leads above.

The gravelled ground, with sleeves tied on the helm,
On foaming horse, with swords and friendly hearts,
With cheer as though the one should overwhelm,
Where we have fought and chasèd oft with darts.

With silver drops the meads yet spread for ruth,
In active games of nimbleness and strength
Where we did strain, trailèd by swarms of youth,
Our tender limbs, that yet shot up in length.

The secret groves, which oft we made resound
Of pleasant plaint and of our ladies' praise,
Recording soft what grace each one had found,
What hope of speed, what dread of long delays.

The wild forest, the clothèd holts with green,
With reins availed and swift ybreathèd horse,
With cry of hounds and merry blasts between,
Where we did chase the fearful hart a force.

The void walls eke, that harboured us each night;
Wherewith, alas, revive within my breast
The sweet accord, such sleeps as yet delight,
The pleasant dreams, the quiet bed of rest,

The secret thoughts imparted with such trust,
The wanton talk, the diverse change of play,
The friendship sworn, each promise kept so just,
Wherewith we passed the winter nights away.

And with this thought the blood forsakes my face,
The tears berain my cheek of deadly hue;
The which, as soon as sobbing sighs, alas,
Upsuppèd have, thus I my plaint renew:

'O place of bliss, renewer of my woes,
Give me accompt where is my noble fere,
Whom in thy walls thou didst each night enclose,
To other lief, but unto me most dear.'

Each stone, alas, that doth my sorrow rue,
Returns thereto a hollow sound of plaint.
Thus I alone, where all my freedom grew,
In prison pine with bondage and restraint,

And with remembrance of the greater grief,
To banish the less I find my chief relief.

'The Windsor Sonnet' has the temper of despair. The poet leans his 'restless head' to view the springtime scene below him, only to find himself considering his loss, 'the heavy charge of care' which is the inescapable legacy of his friend's death. Through the composition of the sonnet, Surrey's art transcends his tears.[21]

When Windsor walls sustained my wearied arm,
My hand my chin, to ease my restless head,
Each pleasant spot revested green with warm,
The blossomed boughs with lusty ver yspread,
The flowered meads, the wedded birds so late
Mine eyes discovered. Then did to mind resort
The jolly woes, the hateless short debate,
The rakehell life that 'longs to love's disport.
Wherewith, alas, mine heavy charge of care
Heaped in my breast, broke forth against my will,
And smoky sighs that overcast the air.
My vapoured eyes such dreary tears distill,
The tender spring to quicken where they fall,
And I half bent to throw me down withal.

A month after the death of his grandfather, the second Duke, the eight-year-old Surrey had accompanied the funeral cortège on its journey from the 'grimly impregnable'[22]Howard castle at Framlingham to Thetford Priory, where were buried the lords of Norfolk. Before he built Mount Surrey, his palace on St Leonard's Hill overlooking the River Wensum in Norwich, much of Surrey's life was a regular progress between Howard houses in East Anglia. At Kenninghall, near Thetford, completed by his father on the site of an earlier house,[23]Surrey was an unwilling dependent. There were residences at Tendring Hall (by the River Stour), Stoke Nayland and Shottisham in Suffolk and, close to Norwich, at the home in Horsham St Faith of the Dowager Duchess. Amongst Howard houses in the city itself, was the fine one his father named after him in Newgate (now Surrey Street).

Mount Surrey was designed to impress. The poet's biographer posits the 'novelty' of its commanding topography as 'reveal[ing] a daring aesthetic dimension'[24]more than two centuries before the Romantics embraced the sublimity of height. On its promontory, where a Roman fortress once guarded the road from Yarmouth, it was no doubt viewed from below as a masterpiece of aggrandizement. Indeed, according to a clause of the indictment brought at Surrey's trial by Thomas Wriothesley, the Lord Chancellor, its military crenellations were intended 'to overawe the city'.[25]Notable features were a dominant bell-tower, possibly of 'a Gothic...shape',[26] and a 'fortress-like gateway'.[27]

Banners displaying his arms and the Howard emblem of a silver lion were regular symbols of his presence in the city as he passed along Bishopsgate to cross the Wensum. The paramount symbol of Surrey's authority, however, was his chair of state 'of purple

16

velvet and satin, embroidered with *passement* silver and gold lace'[28] from which – beyond contradiction – he directed aspects of regional administration. He managed the Duchy of Lancaster's lands in Norfolk, Suffolk and Cambridgeshire and held an onerous brief as a commissioner for sea defences. However, the choicest political goal was to elude him: the future governance of the young Prince Edward (later Edward VI). With Henry VIII's death on 28th January 1547, that glittering prize went to the Earl of Hertford as Lord Protector, to Lisle and to William Paget, Henry's principal secretary. Hertford and others were to take possession of Mount Surrey's finest contents. Of Mount Surrey house itself, nothing remains; its ransacking was completed in 1549 when Kett's rebels, intent on besieging the city, made it their headquarters and prison-house.

Paraphrase of Ecclesiastes, Chapter Two

From pensive fancies then, I gan my heart revoke,
And gave me to such sporting plays as laughter might provoke,
But even such vain delights, when they most blinded me,
Always methought with smiling grace a king did ill agree.
Then sought I how to please my belly with much wine,
To feed me fat with costly feasts of rare delights and fine,
And other pleasures eke, to purchase me with rest,
In so great choice to find the thing that might content me best.
But, Lord, what care of mind, what sudden storms of ire,
With broken sleeps endurèd I, to compass my desire!
To build my houses fair then set I all my cure:
By princely acts thus strove I still to make my fame endure.
Delicious gardens eke I made to please my sight,
And graft therein all kinds of fruits that might my mouth delight.
Conduits, by lively springs, from their old course I drew
For to refresh the fruitful trees that in my garden grew.
Of cattle great increase I bred in little space.
Bondmen I bought, I gave them wives, and served me with their race.
Great heaps of shining gold by sparing gan I save,
With things of price so furnishèd as fits a prince to have.
To hear fair women sing sometime I did rejoice,
Ravishèd with their pleasant tunes and sweetness of their voice.
Lemans I had, so fair and of so lively hue
That who so gazèd in their face might well their beauty rue.
Never erst sat there king so rich in David's seat:
Yet still methought for so small gain the travail was too great.
From my desirous eyes I hid no pleasant sight,
Nor from my heart no kind of mirth that might give them delight;
Which was the only fruit I reaped of all my pain:
To feed my eyes and to rejoice my heart with all my gain.
But when I made my compt, with how great care of mind
And heart's unrest that I had sought so wasteful fruit to find,
Then was I stricken straight with that abusèd fier,
To glory in that goodly wit that compassed my desire.
But fresh before my eyes grace did my faults renew;
What gentle callings I had fled, my ruin to pursue,

What raging pleasures past, peril and hard escape,
What fancies in my head had wrought the liquor of the grape.
The error then I saw that their frail hearts doth move,
Which strive in vain for to compare with him that sits above;
In whose most perfect works such craft appeareth plain
That to the least of them there may no mortal hand attain.
And like as lightsome day doth shine above the night,
So dark to me did folly seem, and wisdom's beams as bright.
Whose eyes did seem so clear, motes to discern and find;
But will had closèd folly's eyes which gropèd like the blind.
Yet death and time consume all wit and worldly fame,
And look what end that folly hath, and wisdom hath the same.
Then said I thus: Oh Lord, may not thy wisdom cure
The wailful wrongs and hard conflicts that folly doth endure?
To sharp my wits so fine then why took I this pain?
Now find I well this noble search may eke be callèd vain.
As slander's loathsome bruit sounds folly's just reward,
Is put to silence all by time, and brought in small regard;
Even so doth time devour the noble blast of fame,
Which should resound their glories great that do deserve the same.
Thus present changes chase away the wonders past,
Nor is the wise man's fatal thread yet longer spun to last.
Then in this wretchèd vale of life I loathèd plain
When I beheld our fruitless pains to compass pleasures vain.
My travail this avail hath me producèd, lo!
An heir unknown shall reap the fruit that I in seed did sow.
But whereunto the Lord his nature shall incline
Who can foreknow, into whose hands I must my goods resign?
But, Lord, how pleasant sweet then seemed the idle life,
That never chargèd was with care, nor burdenèd with strife;
And vile the greedy trade of them that toil so sore
To leave to such their travail's fruit that never sweat therefore.
What is that pleasant gain, which is that sweet relief,
That should delay the bitter taste that we feel of our grief?
The gladsome days we pass to search a simple gain,
The quiet nights, with broken sleeps, to feed a restless brain.
What hope is left us then, what comfort doth remain?
Our quiet hearts for to rejoice with the fruits of our pain.
If that be true, who may himself so happy call
As I, whose free and sumptuous expense doth shine beyond them all.
Surely it is a gift and favour of the Lord
Liberally to spend our goods, the ground of all discord;
And wretchèd hearts have they that let their treasures mould,
And carry the rod that scourgeth them that glory in their gold.
But I do know by proof, whose riches bear such bruit,
What stable wealth may stand in waste by heaping of such fruit.

The poet Earl created at Mount Surrey an aristocratic academy in the manner of Fontainebleau.[29] His audiences, attended by poets (such as Wyatt and Challoner) and scholars (such as Leland, Cheke and Hadrianus Junius), produced poetic texts which influenced the shaping of England's own Renaissance. Among them was the Devonshire Manuscript containing transcriptions of love lyrics – many of them experimental – which, unusually, members of Surrey's circle had first inserted between its blank pages.[30] The later appearance of Tottel's *Miscellany* (1557), in which Surrey himself is represented, was as revolutionary as the Wordsworth-Coleridge collaboration in the *Lyrical Ballads* of 1798.[31]

The blank verse form which Surrey gave to English poetry in his translation of two books of Virgil's *Aeneid* was entirely of his own invention. Its structure of ten syllables and four or five stresses within the unrhymed lines produces an effect of apt felicity whether employed in 'narrative, conversation or soliloquy'; it has 'The kind of sound our sentences would make/If only we could leave them to themselves'.[32] Indeed, Surrey's poetry has been praised for this fine integrity. Declaring the poet Earl to be England's first classical poet, the critic Joseph Warton (1722-1800) welcomed 'his justness of thought, correctness of style and purity of expression'.[33]

> Aeneas with that vision stricken down,
> Well near bestraught, upstart his hair for dread;
> Amid his throat his voice likewise gan stick.
> For to depart by flight he longeth now,
> And the sweet land to leave, astonished sore
> With this advice and message of the gods.
> What may he do, alas? Or by what words
> Dare he persuade the raging queen [Dido] in love?
> Or in what sort may he his tale begin?
> Now here, now there, his reckless mind gan run,
> And diversely him draws, discoursing all.
> (*Aeneid* Book IV, ll.359-369)

As affronts to his nobility, both real and imagined, left Surrey prey to hubris, so it was a matter of heraldic display which duly invited nemesis. Included in his indictment for treason was the charge that, together with his own arms, he had displayed (in the first quarter) those of Edward the Confessor, which 'uniquely belong to and appertain to' Henry VIII and his successors. What is more, the arms – described as 'azure, a cross fleury, between five martlets gold' – were 'by three labels silver' similarly differenced from the king's as were, rightfully, those of his heir.[34] First seen at Kenninghall, these presumptuous arms appeared also at Mount Surrey in glass panels and upon items of silver.[35]

Surrey was committed to the Tower, so often the prison of lost causes, on 12th December 1546. Of the numerous political factors considered by Surrey's enemies in drawing up the dispositions to secure his conviction for being a threat to the throne, none proved as telling as the treasonable heraldic charge. Found 'guilty on the basis of intent',[36] the poet Earl of Surrey was beheaded at Tower Hill on 19th January 1547.

Thomas Tusser ?1524-1580

The maxims of good husbandry for which Thomas Tusser is known did not serve to secure his own livelihood. As Wit's *Recreations* (1641) puts it:

> Tusser, they tell me, when thou wert alive,
> Thou teaching thrift, thyself could never thrive,
> So like the whetstone, many men are wont,
> To sharpen others, when themselves are blunt.

Far from being the distilled wisdom of a lifetime spent with soil between the fingers, *A Hundreth Goode Pointes of Husbandrie* (1557) was the remarkable harvest of a mere four years of 'losse and paine' spent farming above the saltings of the Stour valley at Cattiwade, near Manningtree. By 1573 the advice had been expanded to become *Five Hundreth Pointes of Good Husbandry united to as many of Good Huswifery*, to which was added a verse autobiography. In worldly terms, however, 'this stone of Sisyphus', as Thomas Fuller called Tusser in *The History of the Worthies of England*, 'could gather no moss'.[1]

Malaria, and the sickness of his childless first wife – the most compelling of the circumstances which required Tusser to come to terms with change in the course of his life – hastened a move inland to Ipswich, where his wife died.[2] When he embarked upon a second marriage, in 1559, to Amy Moone ('a Moone of cheerfull hew'), and re-settled in West Dereham, he was soon lamenting that 'for pleasure rare, such endless care,/ hath husband wun'. And he worried that the four sons and daughter Amy bore him 'rob[bed] the purse'. He lived in the precincts of the dissolved Premonstratensian abbey, constantly troubled by the quarrelling of his landlords.[3] In due course, he found a patron in the courtier Sir Richard Southwell, but the death of 'that Jewell great' (in 1564) meant a further uprooting, this time to Norwich.

Through the good offices of John Salisbury, then in his second period of office as Dean of the Cathedral, Tusser joined the choir as a lay clerk.[4] His was a well-trained voice from boyhood when, at the insistence of his father, he was sent as a chorister to the collegiate chapel of Wallingford Castle in Berkshire. 'What [pulled] ears?...What [pouting] lips?', he recalls of this time of unallayed misery; 'What robes, how bare? What college fare? What bread how stale?' At St Paul's in London, however, under the distinguished musician, John Redford, Tusser was grateful to have gained 'some part of Musicke art'.

It was probably Salisbury ('Thou gentle deane') who was instrumental in bringing about yet a further change in Tusser's affairs. He had been unwell in Norwich from a stoppage of the bladder so severe that 'in 138 houres I never made drop of water'. 'From Norwich aire...To seeke more helth' he went to Fairstead in Essex. He had found a position farming the glebe lands there.

The Author's Life

> ...As in this booke, who list to looke,
> Of husbandrie, and huswiferie,
> There may he finde more of my minde,
>   concerning this:
> To carke and care, and ever bare,
> With losse and paine, to little gaine,
> All this to have, to cram sir knave,
>   what life it is.

At Kate-wade in Suffolke this booke first devised.

When wife could not, through sicknes got,
More toile abide, so nigh Sea side,
Then thought I best, from toile to rest, *Ipswich*
    and Ipswich trie: *commenced.*
A towne of price, like paradice,
For quiet then, and honest men,
There was I glad, much friendship had,
    a time to lie.

There left good wife this present life, *The deth of*
And there left I, house charges lie, *his first wife.*
For glad was he, mought send for me,
    good lucke so stood:
In Suffolke there, were everie where,
Even of the best, besides the rest,
That never did their friendship hid,
    to doo me good.

O Suffolke thow, content thee now, *Newe*
That hadst the praies in those same daies, *maried in*
For Squiers and Knights, that well delights *Norfolk.*
    good house to keepe:
For Norfolke wiles, so full of giles,
Have caught my toe, by wiving so,
That out to thee, I see for mee,
    no waie to creepe.

For lo, through gile, what haps the while, *Mistres*
Through Venus toies, in hope of joies, *Amie*
I chanced soone to finde a Moone, *Moone.*
    of cheerfull hew:
Which well a fine me thought did shine,
Did never change, a thing most strange,
Yet kept in sight, hir course aright,
    and compas trew.

Behold of truth, with wife in youth, *The charges*
For joie at large, what daily charge, *following a*
Through childrens hap, what opened gap, *yoong wife.*
    to more begun.
The childe at nurse, to rob the purse.
The same to wed, to trouble hed.
For pleasure rare, such endlesse care,
    hath husband wun.

Then did I dwell in Diram sell,   *West*
A place for wood, that trimlie stood,   *Diram*
With flesh and fish, as heart would wish: *Abbie.*
        but when I spide
That Lord with Lord could not accord,
But now pound he, and now pound we,
Then left I all, bicause such brall,
        I list not bide.

O Soothwell, what meanst thou by that,   *Sir Richarde*
Thou worthie wight, thou famous knight,   *Soothwell.*
So me to crave, and to thy grave,
        go by and by?
O death thou fo, why didst thou so
Ungently treat that Jewell great,
Which opte his doore to rich and poore,
        so bounteously?

There thus bestad, when leave I had,
By death of him, to sinke or swim,
And ravens I saw togither draw,   *His vii*
        in such a sort: *executors.*
Then waies I saught, by wisdome taught,
To beare low saile, least stock should quaile,
Till ship mought finde, with prosperous winde,
        some safer port.

At length by vew, to shore I drew,
Discharging straight both ship and fraight,
At Norwich fine, for me and mine,   *Norwich*
        a citie trim: *Citie.*
Where strangers wel may seeme to dwel,   *Norwich*
That pitch and pay, or keepe their day,   *qualities.*
But who that want, shall find it scant
        so good for him.

But Salisburie how were kept my vow,   *Maister*
If praise from thee were kept by mee,   *Salisburie*
Thou gentle deane, mine onely meane,   *deane of*
        there then to live?   *Norwich.*
Though churles such some to crave can come,
And pray once got, regard thee not,
Yet live or die, so will not I,
        example give.

When learned men could there nor then,   *In 138*
Devise to swage the stormie rage,   *houres I*
Nor yet the furie of my dissurie,   *never made*
        that long I had: *drop of water.*

22

From Norwich aire, in great despaire,
Away to flie, or else to die,
To seeke more helth, to seeke more welth,
    then was I glad.

From thence so sent, away I went,
With sicknes worne, as one forlorne,
To house my hed, at Faiersted,   *Fairsted*
    where whiles I dwelt: *parsonage*
The tithing life, the tithing strife,   *in Essex.*
Through tithing ill, of Jacke and Gill,
The dailie paies, the mierie waies,
    too long I felt.

More arable man than grazier, Tusser was sanguine about the tide of enclosures that was bringing communally-owned open-fields (champion) under individual ownership (severalty)[5] – a matter which helped to provoke Kett's Norfolk rising in 1549. He knew that 'champion countrie' wasted enterprise. 'When thou hast bestowed thy cost', he complains, 'looke halfe of the same to be lost' – not least through over-cropping and the casual intrusion of farm stock:

In Norfolke behold the dispaire
    of tillage too much to be borne:
By drovers from faire to faire,
    and others destroieng the corne.
By custome and covetous pates,
    by gaps, and by opening of gates.

Tusser was not without farming ideas of his own at a time of slowly evolving agricultural practice, when the countryside was beginning to show the familiar chequer pattern of hedge and covert which today is increasingly supplanted.[6] He recommends a three-crop rather than the common two-crop and fallow rotation, choosing (except for beans) a thick seeding to discourage weeds which, owing to enclosure, were not so much required for early winter grazing. Indeed, for the purpose of suppressing weeds, Tusser was prepared to plough fallow three times.[7] With root crops not yet introduced, he needed to manage winter feed for housed livestock with great care. Stock were fed rye and wheat straws and pea haulm first, then oat and barley straws, and hay last, lest 'they love not straw, they had rather to fast'.[8]

Amongst the wealth of sage advice can be found items of near whimsy. For example, fruit gatherers pick their crop to last, only under a waning moon, whereas fine seeds are sown 'whilst Moone doth growe'. And to provide dry places for lambs to lie in damp pasture, molehills should be left unlevelled.[9]

For each month of his calendar, Tusser provides its embodiment in verse, sayings of which a few have passed into folklore. To him we owe 'Feb[ruary], fill the dyke/ With what thou dost like', as well as 'Sweet April showers/Do spring May flowers'.

'Huswifelie matters have never an end', coined Tusser in *The Pointes of Huswiferie*, and bequeathed a dictum which discomforts our age. Domestic harmony, it seems, is the housewife's gift to bestow and requires her virtuous attention to unflagging routines: 'As order is heavenly where quiet is had', he avers, 'so error is hell, or a mischief as bad'.

Regular mealtimes are essential. 'Dinner' should be ready at noon, for 'let meate tarrie servant, not servant his meate'. Tusser's preponderant concern, however, is to avoid waste of any kind. Those who 'gnaweth and leaveth, some crusts and some crums' should 'eat such their own levings, or gnaw their own thums'; moreover, a covered table is wasted on those who cut the linen or spill their broth. In the dairy where 'scouring is needfull', an excess of it 'is pride without profit, and robbeth thine linen or spill their broth. In the dairy where 'scouring is needfull', an excess of it 'is pride without profit, and robbeth thine hutch'. And in the kitchen all 'droppings and skimmings' must be saved 'for medcine for cattell, for cart and for shoo.'

Stern discipline is tempered by an understanding of the workers' lot. Though it is necessary to 'shew servant his labour, and shew him no more', the housewife should 'distaine not the honest though merie they seeme'. It is well, Tusser says, that good servants 'sing in their labour, as birdes in thee wood' and that labourers are 'merie all haruest long.'

Conjugal wisdom abounds. 'Love so as ye may/Love many a day', appreciates Tusser and knows what a blessing is a wife's aptitude for accommodation: 'Be lowly not sollen, if ought go amisse,/what wrestling may loose thee, that winne with a kisse'. Above all, he seeks to avoid the bane of conflict: 'Both beare and forebeare now and then as ye may', he presses, 'then, wench God a mercie, thy husband will say.'

Morning Workes

No sooner some up,
But nose is in cup.
Get up in the morning as soone as thou wilt,
with overlong slugging good servant is split.

Some slovens from sleeping no sooner get up,
but hand is in aumbrie, and nose in the cup.

That early is donne,
Count huswifely wonne.
Some worke in the morning may trimly be donne,
that all the day after can hardly be wonne.

Good husband without it is needfull there be,
good huswife within as needfull as he.

Cast dust into yard,
And spin and go card.
Sluts corners avoided shall further thy health,
much time about trifles shall hinder thy wealth.

Set some to peele hempe or else rishes to twine,
to spin and to card, or to seething of brine.

Grind mault for drinke,
See meate do not stinke.
Set some about cattle, some pasture to vewe,
some mault to be grinding against ye do brewe.

24

Some corneth, some brineth, some will not be taught,
where meate is attainted, there cookrie is naught.

To breakefast that come,
Give erie one some.
Call servants to breakefast by day starre appere,
a snatch and to worke, fellowes tarrie not here.

Let huswife be carver, let potage be heate,
a messe to eche one, with a morsell of meate.

No more tittle tattle,
Go serve your cattle.
What tacke in a pudding, saith greedie gut wringer,
give such ye wote what, ere a pudding he finger.

Let servants once served, they cattle go serve,
least often ill serving make cattle to sterve.

Fuller, who believed that there was 'none...better at the theory or worse at the practice' of husbandry than Tusser, had the true measure of him. Thomas Tusser ended his days in London, a prisoner for debt in the Poultry counter, where he died on 3rd May 1580.

The Ladder of Thrift

To take thy calling thankfully,
  and shun the path to beggery.
To grudge in youth no drudgery,
  to come by knowledge perfectly.
To count no travell slaverie,
  that brings in penie saverlie.
To folow profit earnestlie,
  but meddle not with pilferie.
To get by honest practisie,
  and keepe thy gettings covertlie.
To lash not out too lashinglie,
  for feare of pinching penurie.
To get good plot to occupie,
  and store and use it husbandlie.
To shew to landlord curtesie,
  and keepe thy covenants orderlie.
To hold that thine is lawfullie,
  for stoutnes or for flatterie.
To wed good wife for companie,
  and live in wedlock honestlie.
To furnish house with housholdry,
  and make provision skilfully.
To joine to wife good familie,
  and none to keepe for braverie.

To suffer none live idlelie,
  for feare of idle knaverie.
To courage wife in huswiferie,
  and use well dooers gentilie.
To keepe no more but needfullie,
  and count excesse unsaverie.
To raise betimes the lubberlie,
  both snorting Hob and Margerie.
To walke thy pastures usuallie,
  to spie ill neighbours subtiltie.
To hate revengement hastilie,
  for loosing love and amitie.
To love thy neighbour neighborly,
  and shew him no discurtesy.
To answere stranger civilie,
  but shew him not thy secresie.
To use no friend deceitfully,
  to offer no man villeny.
To learne how foe to pacifie,
  but trust him not too trustilie.
To keepe thy touch substanciallie,
  and in thy word use constancie.
To make thy bandes advisedly,
  and com not bound through suerty.
To meddle not with usurie,
  nor lend thy monie foolishlie.
To hate to live in infamie,
  through craft, and living shiftingly.
To shun all kinde of treachery,
  for treason endeth horribly.
To learne to eschew ill company,
  and such as live dishonestly.
To banish house of blasphemie,
  least crosses crosse unluckelie.
To stop mischance, through policy,
  for chancing too unhappily.
To beare thy crosses paciently,
  for worldly things are slippery.
To laie to keepe from miserie,
  age comming on so creepinglie.
To praie to God continuallie,
  for aide against thine enimie.
To spend thy Sabboth holilie,
  and helpe the needie povertie.
To live in conscience quietly,
  and keepe thy selfe from malady.
To ease thy sicknes speedilie,
  ere helpe be past recoverie.

To seeke to God for remedie,
  for witches proove unluckilie.
These be the steps unfainedlie:
  to climbe to thrift by husbandrie.

These steps both reach, and teach thee shall:
To come to thrift, to shift withall.

Robert Greene 1558-1592

In a pamphlet he called *Repentance*, written shortly before his death, Robert Greene laid bare the dissolute course of his student years at Cambridge: 'I light amongst wags as lewd as my selfe,' he said of his friends, 'with whome I consumed the flower of my youth'.[1] On a tour in their company to the Continent, such yearning as was theirs for what Erasmus, while in Rome, had treasured as 'sweet confabulation with the learned', was apt to fade. When, for example, Greene spoke of Venetian scholars that they met, he admitted that 'as our wits be as ripe as any, so our willes are more ready than they all, to put into effect any of their licentious abuses'.[2]

We can picture Greene and his companions newly disembarked in Venice from one of the passenger boats which plied daily from the university city of Padua.[3] He wears his silks, and sports the red beard he so cherished, and which (according to his friend, the writer Thomas Nashe), 'was so sharp and pendant' that from it a man might choose to hang a jewel.[4] So he proceeds in jovial company along streets 'so clean that you [could] walk in a Silk Stockin and Sattin Slippes',[5] and amongst upstart courtiers whom he later parodied for wearing fine pearl lace 'which scarce Caligula wore on his birthday'.[6] Amorous ones cast 'eggs into the wyndowes among the ladies full of sweete waters and damaske Poulders'.[7] And soon, drawn to balconied rooms, Greene himself yields further to the 'foreign vices' of which he and his companions so freely brag.

He returned to England a 'Malcontent', took his degree, and moved to London to a life of 'grave irregularities'. He began to write in haste, first – in the new Elizabethan genre of fiction – the didactic *Mamillia*, a story of two faithful women's constancy to a faithless man. There followed a series of pamphlets which treat of the pleasures and sufferings of love. He was pandering unashamedly to fashion as, all the while, dissipation consumed his earnings.

On a visit (c.1585) to Norwich, the place of his birth, there occurred an episode with power to break the mould. Greene found himself greatly moved to hear a local preacher (in St Andrew's church) contrast the misery of sinners with the joys of the godly; he left the church convinced that he too must walk in the way of righteousness. But he could not stomach the laughter of his friends. 'This good motion,' he said, 'lasted not long in mee.'

In Norwich, also, Greene knew conjugal happiness – but for barely a year – before his love turned cold at his wife's reproaches. Dorothy, a squire's daughter 'of good account' from Lincolnshire, bore him a son. Restless hedonism and the pulse of family life were irreconcilable; after spending her dowry, he deserted her and returned with his son to London.

In Greene's pastoral romance, *Menaphon* (1589), there is a fine cradle-song, a form found rarely in Elizabethan poetry. Written, in all probability, with the memory of past love not yet staled, it may prompt in the reader, perhaps, recollection of a husband's reflective stillness in the presence of maternal joy and sighings.

Sephestia's Song To Her Child

Weep not, my wanton, smile upon my knee;
When thou art old there's grief enough for thee.
   Mother's wag, pretty boy,
   Father's sorrow, father's joy.

When thy father first did see
Such a boy by him and me,
He was glad, I was woe,
Fortune changed made him so,
When he left his pretty boy
Last his sorrow, first his joy.

.Weep not, my wanton, smile upon my knee,
When thou art old there's grief enough for thee.
Streaming tears that never stint,
Like pearl drops from a flint,
Fell by course from his eyes,
That one another's place supplies;
Thus he grieved in every part,
Tears of blood fell from his heart,
When he left his pretty boy,
Father's sorrow, father's joy.

Weep not, my wanton, smile upon my knee,
When thou art old there's grief enough for thee.
The wanton smiled, father wept,
Mother cried, baby leapt;
More he crowed, more we cried,
Nature could not sorrow hide:
He must go, he must kiss
Child and mother, baby bless,
For he left his pretty boy,
Father's sorrow, father's joy.

Weep not, my wanton, smile upon my knee,
When thou art old there's grief enough for thee.

A series of what have been called 'prodigal-son' stories confirmed Greene's growing disillusion with writing which merely entertained; in future, he would employ his pen to moral purpose. He considered *Mourning Garment* (1590), which follows closely the pattern of the prodigal's story (in St Luke's Gospel), the 'fruit of my new labours and the last farewell to my fond desires'.[8] An admirer was unequivocal in his judgment: Greene's writings, he acknowledged, 'never gave the looser cause to laugh,/Ne men of judgment for to be offended.'[9]

Mourning Garment tells of a handsome youth, Philador, who, on leaving his father's house 'is beguiled by rapacious courtesans' in distant Thessaly.[10] Like St Luke's prodigal, he is reduced to penury, assures his survival during a famine by eating the husks fed to swine, and returns to his father a penitent. Because Greene's employment of the theme of repentance is in keeping with a popular convention in Elizabethan literature, it does not, of itself, justify the reading of the story as an allegorical representation of his life. Even so, Greene has compared himself (in the book's dedication) to the wicked city of Nineveh newly awakened from its sinful ways through the preaching of the prophet Jonah.[11] What is more, in placing Philador in the company of shepherds living in pastoral 'sweet content', and ignorant still of the women who are to be his downfall, we can imagine Greene – in his abandon – dwelling upon the painful loss of uncorrupted love that knows 'such sweet desires'.

The Shepherd's Wife's Song

Ah, what is love? It is a pretty thing,
As sweet unto a shepherd as a king;
    And sweeter too,
For kings have cares that wait upon a crown,
And cares can make the sweetest love to frown:
    Ah then, ah then,
If country loves such sweet desires do gain,
What lady would not love a shepherd swain?

His flocks are folded, he comes home at night,
As merry as a king in his delight;
    And merrier too,
For kings bethink them what the state require,
Where shepherds careless carol by the fire:
    Ah then, ah then,
If country loves such sweet desires do gain,
What lady would not love a shepherd swain?

He kisseth first, then sits as blithe to eat
His cream and curds, as doth the king his meat;
    And blither too,
For kings have often fears when they do sup,
Where shepherds dread no poison in their cup:
    Ah then, ah then,
If country loves such sweet desires do gain,
What lady would not love a shepherd swain?

To bed he goes, as wanton then, I ween,
As is a king in dalliance with a queen;
    More wanton too,
For kings have many griefs affects to move,
Where shepherds have no greater grief than love:
    Ah then, ah then,
If country loves such sweet desires do gain,
What lady would not love a shepherd swain?

Upon his couch of straw he sleeps as sound,
As doth the king upon his bed of down;
    More sounder too,
For cares cause kings full oft their sleep to spill,
Where weary shepherds lie and snort their fill:
    Ah then, ah then,
If country loves such sweet desires do gain,
What lady would not love a shepherd swain?

Thus with his wife he spends the year, as blithe
As doth the king at every tide or sith;
        And blither too,
For kings have wars and broils to take in hand,
When shepherds laugh and love upon the land:
        Ah then, ah then,
If country loves such sweet desires do gain,
What lady would not love a shepherd swain?

Greene freely associated with members of London's underworld. We know that the mother of his illegitimate child, Fortunatus, was sister to the wife of 'Cutting Ball', a notorious leader of a gang of thieves, who was hanged at Tyburn. And with an eye to pecuniary gain, Greene exposed criminal practices in knowing detail through a series of pamphlets published in the face of threats to his person.

He brought to light the astonishing plethora of trickery that was the undoing of naïve visitors and citizens alike; no bystander, or country fellow 'in coat of homespun russet'[12] caught up in the throng of the most crowded city in Europe, could safely presume the innocence of those who jostled them. In *A Notable Discovery of Cozenage* Greene introduces the full range of characters, notably the pickpockets, cutpurses, 'cozeners' (cheats) and card-sharpers of the narrow ways, the taverns, the playhouses, the bowling alleys and stews (brothels). 'Cony-catchers' (tricksters) lure 'gulls' (dupes) to their haunt, where they are 'fair game for the nip [cutpurse] and foist [pickpocket] as well as for the punk [whore] and the pimp'.[13]

Greene was ever the opportunist, quick to exploit whatever literary genre was in fashion. As dramatist, for example, he was ambitious to emulate the success of Marlowe, who was a close friend. But his plays are largely imitative: *Orlando Furioso* parodies the use of madness on the stage in Thomas Kyd's popular *Spanish Tragedy*, while *The Comical History of Alphonsus, King of Arragon*, has been called Marlowe's '*Tambur-laine* emasculated'.[14]Only in the later plays, *Friar Bacon* and *James IV*, is there 'originality and gain'.[15](About Shakespeare, Greene was simply ungracious, calling him 'an upstart crow dressed in our feathers'.)[16]

At the age of thirty-four, Greene's abused constitution succumbed after a night of carousing, and its dinner of pickled herring and Rhenish wine. He returned to lodgings he rented on credit from a poor shoemaker and his wife. Only two visitors called in the time left to him, one of whom was his former mistress. At his death, Mrs Isam, the shoemaker's wife, wreathed him with a garland of bay leaves, as he had requested.

The last letter Greene had received brought commendations from his wife. He penned his reply, supplicating her to 'forget and forgive my wronge done unto thee'.[17]

Menaphon's Song

Some say, Love,
Foolish Love
        Doth rule and govern all the Gods;
I say Love,
Inconstant Love,
        Sets men's senses far at odds.

31

Some swear Love,
Smooth-faced Love,
    Is sweetest sweet that men can have:
I say, Love,
Sour Love,
    Makes virtue yield as beauty's slave:

A bitter sweet, a folly worst of all,
That forceth wisdom to be folly's thrall...

John Taylor, the Water Poet 1580-1653

John Taylor found his first audience among the actors and writers whom he ferried for a living between the City and the Bankside playhouses in Southwark. No doubt they found him 'very facetious and diverting company' as John Aubrey acknowledged in *Brief Lives*, having met him in Oxford during the Civil War. 'For stories and lively telling them, few could out-do him.'[1] And mid-stream on the Thames, Taylor would press them to consider his writings with their titles of calculated oddity.

His first collection – of scattered verses – he called: *The Sculler, Rowing from Tiber to Thames, with his Boate laden with a hotch potch, or Gallimawfrey of Sonnets, Satyres, and Epigrams*. There is the bizarrely titled: *The Scourge of Basenesse: or, the old Lerry, with a new Kicksey, and a new-cum twang, with the old Winsey*, and the paradoxical one, *A Bawd, a vertuous Bawd*. And he is responsible for the schoolmaster's composition title of last resort: *A Shilling or, Travailles of Twelve-pence.*[2]

Taylor was a literary chameleon. He strove to cultivate the good opinion of the educated élite through hard-won learning, while pandering to vulgar taste with 'artless' ease. Of Cromer folk he wrote:

> So all amazed were all these senseless blocks,
> That had the town been fired, it is a doubt,
> But that the women there had pissed it out,
> And from the men reeked such a fearful scent,
> That people three mile thence mused what it meant.[3]

'Though my lines no scholarship proclaim,' the poet once admitted, 'yet I at learning have a kind of aim.'[4] He was a reader of the classics in translation, and among English writers, peppering texts with references and allusions. And he culled his work *Misselanies, or, Fifty Years Gatherings* (1652) from a lifetime's selections in a commonplace book. But the vein of hubris is constantly exposed. He is amused to cite fake authorities, for example the Utopian philosopher Nymshag for 'his treatise of the antiquity of ginger-bread, Lib.7, pag. 30,000'.[5] In a marginal note, the zoological works of Gesner and Pliny are mentioned as being 'books which I never read'.[6] And a book of nonsense is given a spoof bibliography.[7] Fellow writers could be cruelly dismissive. When in a contemporary play a student requests an item of Taylor's 'nonsense' ('Sir Gregory Nonsense'), the servant quips, 'you mean all his works, sir.'[8]

In the spirit of Will Kemp's morris-dance from London to Norwich in 1599, Taylor made a number of whimsical journeys of his own. He funded them by inviting sponsorship through the issue of prospectuses to distinguished patrons – 'Taylor's bills' he called them. So consummate was the self-publicity that in 1618 he was able to complete a journey on foot from London to Edinburgh, and on to Braemar, with no money, yet without need of 'begging, borrowing or asking meat, drink or lodging'.[9]

Watched by thousands of spectators lining the Thames, he set out in a brown-paper boat one summer evening in 1619 with a vintner friend for Quinborough, in Kent. When the bottom fell out, they rowed on, buoyed up only by inflated bladders fastened to the sides. For oars they used two stockfish tied to canes.

John Taylor, the Water Poet

It was on a 'wagering journey' made in 1622, from London to York by way of Hull and the River Ouse, that Taylor was forced by bad weather to make a landfall at Cromer. He met with scurvy treatment at the hands of a fearful populace, the crew being taken for Dunkirkers – pirates who troubled the coast. He claims that:

> The dreadful names of Talbot, or of Drake,
> Ne'er made the foes of England more to quake
> Than I made Cromer;

The gentlest raillery informs the narrative: his sympathy for a town 'unable by expense,/Against the raging sea to make defence' curbs an appetite for irreverence. The town's petition for relief presented to Edward VI in 1551 recorded that coastal erosion had 'swallowed up and drowned a number of great houses.' The heavy-timbered pierhead and harbour walls were in constant need of repair. Moreover, part of the town remained gutted by fire.

The 'goodly' church Taylor admired bore scars of neglect: by 1681 part of the chancel had fallen. A local rector, the Reverend Thomas Gill, received permission to block up the chancel arch and the east ends of the north and south aisles before what remained of the chancel was demolished with gunpowder. The tower, which soars to fifty metres, is second in height in Norfolk to the west tower of Wymondham Abbey.

> And thus half soused, half stewed, with sea and sweat,
> We land at Cromer Town half dry, half wet;
> But we supposing all was safe and well,
> In shunning Scylla on Charybdis fell;
> For why, some women and some children there
> That saw us land, were all possessed with fear;
> And much amaz'd ran crying up and down,
> That enemies were come to take the town.
> Some said that we were pirates, some said thieves,
> And what the women says, the men believes.
> With that four constables did quickly call,
> Your aid! to arms your men of Cromer all.
> Then straightway forty men with rusty bills,
> Some arm'd in ale, all of approved skill,
> Divided into four stout regiments,
> To guard the city from dangerous events.
> Brave Captain Pescod did the vanguard lead,
> And Captain Clarke the rearward governed,
> Whilst Captain Wiseman and hot Captain Kimble,
> Were in main battalia fierce and nimble.
>
> ...Some rascals ran into my boat apace,
> And turn'd and tumbled her, like men of Gotham,
> Quite topsy-turvy upward with her bottom,
> Vowing they would in tatters piece-meal tear
> They cursed pirate's boat, that bred their fear;

And I am sure, their madness (to my harm)
Tore a board out much longer than mine arm.
And they so bruis'd and split our wherry, that
She leaked, we cast out water with a hat.
Now let men judge, upon this truth's revealing,
If Turks or Moors could use more barb'rous dealing;
Or whether it be fit I should not write,
Their envy, foolish fear, and mad despite.
What may wise men conceive, when they shall note,
That five unarmed men in a wherry boat,
Naught to defend, or to offend with stripes,
But one old sword and two tobacco pipes;
And that of constables a murnivall,
Men, women, children, all in general,
And that they all should be so valiant wise,
To fear we would a market town surprise.

...Sweet Mr. Pescod's double diligence,
Had horsed himself to bear intelligence
To justices of peace within the land,
What dangerous business there was now at hand.
There was I forced to tarry all the while,
Till some said he rode four-and-twenty mile,
In seeking men of worship, peace, and quorum,
Most wisely to declare strange news before um.
And whatsoever tales he did recite,
I sure he caused Sir Austin Palgrave, knight,
And Mr. Robert Kemp, a justice there,
Came before me to know how matters were.
As conference 'twixt them and I did pass,
They quickly understood me what I was;
And though they knew me not in prose and looks,
They had read of me in my verse and books.
My businesses account I there did make,
And I and all my company did take
The lawful oath of our allegiance then,
By which we were believed for honest men.

...Besides, Sir Austin Palgrave bade me this,
To go but four miles, where his dwelling is,
And I and all my company should there
Find friendly welcome, mixed with other cheer.
I gave them thanks, and so I'll give them still,
And did accept their cheer in their good will.
Then 3 o'clock at afternoon and past,
I was discharged from Cromer at the last.
But for men should not think that enviously
Against this town I let my lines to fly;

36

Cromer: 'Upon a lofty cliff of mouldring sands'

And that I do not lie, or scoff, or fable,
For then I will write something charitable.
It is an ancient market town that stands
Upon a lofty cliff of mouldring sands;
The sea against the cliffs doth daily beat,
And every tide into the land doth eat.
The town is poor, unable by expense,
Against the raging sea to make defence;
And every day it eateth further in,
Still waiting, washing down the sand doth win,
That if some course be not ta'en speedily,
The town's in danger in the sea to lie.
A goodly church stands on these brittle grounds,
Not many fairer in Great Britain's bounds;
And if the sea shall swallow it as some fear,
'Tis not ten thousand pounds the like could rear.
No Christian can behold it but with grief,
And with my heart I wish them quick relief.
So farewell, Cromer, I have spoke for thee,
Though you did'st much unkindly deal with me...

Richard Corbett 1582-1635

During the course of Richard Corbett's episcopacy at Norwich, the martinet Archbishop Laud (to whom he owed his appointment) chose to rebuke the undergraduates of Cambridge for disporting themselves in lurid stockings. To Corbett, who in temperament was no stickler for the fine detail of Laudian reform, this pedantry may well have brought a *frisson* of wry remembrance. On a warm evening at Christ Church, Oxford, where as a young man he had been enjoying a bout of drinking with fellow students on the college roof, Corbett cut a series of scissor holes in the stockings of a sleeping scholar. 'Perceiving how and by whom he was abused', reports Aubrey in *Brief Lives*, the scholar 'did chastise him, and made him pay for them'.[1]

It was Laud who, as a strenuous fellow of St John's, had excited a faction of high-church dons to dispute with the long-dominant Calvinists within the university – men whose interests were represented by Robert Abbot, the Professor of Divinity, and his brother George (the future Archbishop). For his part, Corbett was no scholar restless for the ether of doctrinal purity, but he held in affection a Church with an ordered past, and treasured its proper observances.[2] In *Iter Boreale*, a poem which celebrates a journey with friends through the Midlands, he is saddened as he visits Banbury (one of the most Puritan towns in England) to see evidence of delapidation:

> ...And on the feast of Barthol'mew wee try
> What Revells that Saint keepes at Banbury.
> In th' name of God Amen, first to begin,
> The Altar was translated to an Inne;
> Wee lodged in a Chappell by the signe,
> But in a banquerupt Taverne by the Wine:
> Besides, our horses usage made us thinke
> 'Twas still a Church, for they in Coffins drinke...

The Crosses also, like old stumps of trees,
Are stooles for horsemen that haue feeble knees;
Carry noe heads aboue ground: They which tell
That Christ hath nere descended into Hell,
But to the Graue, his Picture buried haue
In a far deeper dungeon then a Graue...
(*Iter Boreale*, ll.445-452;487-492)

When Laud's Vicar-General, Sir Nathaniel Brent, carried out an official visitation in the Norwich diocese a month before Corbett's death, he met evidence of church decay at every turn. In Norwich he perceived the contrast between ecclesiastical poverty and the city's merchant wealth.[3]'The cathedral church is much out of order,' he reported. 'The hangings of the choir are naught, the pavement not good, the spire of the steeple is quite down, the copes are fair but want mending, the churchyard is very ill-kept.'[4] There was little decorum, either: a privy was sited at the west end of the nave; and not all of the priests wore vestments.[5] Away from the city – around Fakenham, for instance – many parsonage-houses were found 'ruinous'; at Yarmouth the church roof was 'very ruinous', and the churchyard 'kept very undecently'.[6]

Corbett was a determined careerist. The connections of his Christ Church friends at court were so propitious that the vicissitudes of royal favour caused barely a stumble on the path to high office. When, for example, the Earl of Nottingham and other members of the Howard family fell from power, the learned Sir Thomas Aylesbury, an exact contemporary, was retained in his position of influence as secretary to the new Lord High Admiral, George Villiers, successively Earl, Marquis and Duke of Buckingham.[7] A poetic epistle written to Aylesbury in 1618 addresses him as 'my brother, and much more had'st thou bin mine...'[8] In June 1620 Corbett's place-hunting was rewarded when Buckingham's influence with James I secured his appointment as Dean of Christ Church, Oxford.

By all accounts Corbett was an esteemed wit, and given to enjoyment of jests and caprices, irrespective of the dignity of office. And when he did maintain gravitas, the ridiculous was apt to spoil things. The King, 'who highly valued him for his fine fancy and preaching',[9] once witnessed his antics during the course of a sermon he preached before the court at Woodstock, after his further appointment as a royal chaplain, in 1621. Well launched into the sermon, Corbett's absent-minded twirling of a ring attached to his clerical attire became so much a preoccupation that he lost the thread of his thoughts and fell silent. Soon someone's waggish verses were going the round of the taverns:

A reverend Deane,
With his Ruffe starch't cleane,
Did preach before the King:
In his Band-string was spied
A Ring that was tyed,
Was not that a pritty thing?
The Ring without doubt
Was the thing putt him out,
So oft hee forgot what was next;
For all that were there,
On my conscience dare sweare
That he handled it more than his Text.[10]

39

When an assassin, John Fenton, ended the Duke of Buckingham's hegemony with the thrust of a dagger, Corbett lost his patron, but not before receiving – only ten days earlier – nomination to the Oxford bishopric he so coveted. His bold, albeit calculated, intervention *Against the Opposing the Duke in Parliament, 1628,* which was written amid calls for the Duke's impeachment after a series of military misadventures on the Continent, may well have encouraged the granting of this last service. But, having secured his prize, Corbett soon chafed to find that a bishop's lot during Laud's ascendancy was no sinecure.

Bound now to reside in their dioceses, the bishops were enjoined to prosecute reforms, as Charles I put it, for 'the preservation of True religion'.[11] From Corbett, who was translated to Norwich in 1632, not least for the purpose of harassing Puritans in one of their strongholds, the harsh measures which were expected of him were not forthcoming: he was known for being 'of a courteous carriage' and, disliking contention, showed 'no destructive nature to any who offended him, counting himself plentifully repaired with a jest upon him'.[12]

Despite entreaties, he failed to oust the Dutch and Walloon congregations from the Bishop's Chapel in Norwich. It had been licensed to them in more tolerant times by the Elizabethan bishop, Dr Parkhurst, and there they remained until Matthew Wren, Corbett's successor, proceeded 'passionately and warmly' against them.[13] Corbett suspended Puritan ministers, but rank persecution was not to his taste. At Yarmouth, where 'to the godly nose the very sea-breeze carried a savour of zeal and Amsterdam',[14] a recalcitrant, without fear of hindrance, was allowed to await a favourable tide.

Corbett's wife, Alice, daughter of Dr Leonard Hutten, with whom he shared the journey recorded in *Iter Boreale,* died of smallpox in 1628. They had married only three years earlier. As Bishop in Oxford he relied for companionship upon his chaplains, William Strode, Poet to the University and Public Orator, and Thomas Lushington of Pembroke College, a high-church wit and imbiber. Both chaplains moved with him to Norfolk (where Lushington was appointed to Barton Turf and Neatishead, and Strode to East Bradenham). Aubrey tells how Corbett would retire with Lushington to the wine-cellar. 'The Bishop first lays down his episcopal hat – "There lyes the Bishop." Then he putts off his gowne, – "There lyes the Doctor." Then 'twas, "Here's to thee, Corbet[t]," and "Here's to thee, Lushington".'[15]

Corbett shared the bishop's palace, Ludham Hall, with two motherless children and his mother, Benet, who was slipping into senility.

Certain tru[e] Woords spoken concerning one Benet Corbett after her death; she dyed October the Second Anno 1634

> Here, or not many feet from hence
> The virtue lies call'd Patience.
> Sickness and Death did do her honour
> By loosing paine and feare upon her.
> 'Tis true they forst her to a grave,
> That's all the triumph that they have, –
> A silly one; retreat o'er night
> Proves conquest in a morning fight.
> She will rise up against them both;
> All sleep, believe it, is not sloth.

And thou that read'st her elegie,
Take something of her historie:
She had one husband and one sonne;
Ask who they were, and thou hast done.

Corbett's poetical talent was fostered through a love of popular song. As a young man at
Oxford he exhibited 'a vagabond streak',[16] liking to don the leather jacket common to
ballad-singers who roved in the company of strolling players. Aubrey tells of him at the
cross in Abingdon on market day holding an audience with his 'rare full voice'.[17] In *To the
Lord Mordant* he admits to having 'sung John Dory in my youth' as well as 'Chevy [Chase]
and Arthur and the Siege of Gaunt.'[18] And he prefaces a number of poems with in-
structions as to their rendering: for example, 'The Distracted Puritane' is 'an excellent new
dittie to the tune of Tom o' Bedlam'.[19]

Only once does Corbett depart from the 'rollicking satiric vein'[20] which characterises
his verse when, in response to the approaches of an infatuated Oxford widow, he gives vent
to sustained malice in 'Upon An Unhandsome Gentlewoman, who made Love unto him'.
He said of Mrs Mallett, whom he called 'the Spouse of Antichrist', that 'one kisse of hers...
put downe the Spanish Inquisition'.

Episcopal duties allowed little time for writing poetry. Only the epitaph for his mother,
and an anthem for Trinity Sunday, are thought to belong to Corbett's years at Norwich. His
poems were widely circulated in manuscript, but none (except Latin verses) were printed in
his lifetime.[21]

Corbett is buried in the cathedral at Norwich. He spoke his last words to his chaplain:
'Good night, Lushington,' he said.

For Trinity Sunday, an Anthymne

Blessed forever may he bee,
That doth confess in Persons Three
    One Unity:
Cursed forever bee that Man,
Who not believeth, what Fayth can,
    The Trinity.

One Father sendeth from above,
By his owne Power, Truth and Love;
    These are his beames:
He sendeth us his sonne and Spirit,
To sayle towards him without our Merit,
    These are our Streames.

O holy, holy, holy Lord,
Who beeing One dost Three afford
    Prayse to the Trinity:
Blessed forever may he bee,
That doth confess in Persons Three
    The Unity.

Drawn by G.Clint A.R.A.   Engraved by A.Duncan.

Thomas Shadwell ?1642-1692

At the time of his matriculation, Thomas Shadwell is known to have been living at Broomhill House near Brandon, which was built upon the ruins of Broomhill Priory on the Norfolk side of the Little Ouse, where the parishes of Weeting and Santon meet. His place of birth is taken to have been Santon Hall, one of his father's seats. (The house, on land which is now a Forestry Commission reserve, no longer stands.)

Shadwell's father, John, a man of Royalist sympathies who had to sell much of his property at the time of the Civil War when he had his eleven children to maintain, was able to provide his son with tutors. One of them, John Jenkins, was known in a number of Norfolk houses. He was Musician-in-Ordinary to both Charles I and Charles II and taught Shadwell to play the lute.[1] In writing the libretto for the opera *Psyche* (1675) – with music by Matthew Locke and Giovanni Baptista Draghi – Shadwell admits that he 'did not so much take care of the Wit or Fancy of [the words], as the making of 'em proper for Music'. He had been 'bred for many Years,' he said, 'to the performance of it'.[2] And the poet Tom Brown in one of his *Letters from the Dead to the Living* describes Shadwell 'thrumming upon an old Theorbo' and as one who 'still keeps up his Musical Talent in these gloomy Territories'.[3]

Shadwell attended the King Edward VI Free Grammar School at Bury St Edmunds under the Cavalier headmaster Thomas Stephens, a man 'pedant enough, and noted for high flights of poetry and criticism'. (After the Restoration, he was known for having his pupils dress in cloaks of Charles II's favoured scarlet when he conducted them through the streets to church.)[4] As a 'pensioner to the bachelors' table' at Gonville and Caius College,

Cambridge – then stocked with Parliamentarian Fellows – Shadwell encountered men of dourer conviction. After a mere eighteen months, he left without taking a degree. In July 1658, he entered the Middle Temple. Soon, and before he ever wrote a play, his conversation was held in regard amongst London's theatrical élite.[5]

At a date unknown, Shadwell married a Norwich girl, the actress Anne Gibbs, whose stage career was well established. A daughter of Thomas Gibbs, proctor and public notary in Norwich, she was a member of the Duke's Company, with whom she played Olivia in *Twelfth Night* and Julia in Webster's *Duchess of Malfi*, productions attended by Samuel Pepys. By 1667, 'Mrs. Shadwel[l]' was taking the role of the splenetic Emilia in her husband's first comedy, *The Sullen Lovers; or The Impertinents* (1668). (Of the Shadwells' offspring, Charles was to be the editor of his father's *Works*.)[6]

Shadwell's reputation was destined never to emerge from the shadows cast by John Dryden's criticism of him. And to those who indulged a taste for censorious discourse in the coffee-houses of Caroline London, Dryden's unsparing language would not have been thought excessive.[7] As the character Og in *Absalom and Achitophel*, Shadwell is an obese imbiber; in *MacFlecknoe* he is dismissed as one 'mature in dullness',[8] a man 'confirm'd in full stupidity' who 'never deviates into sense'.[9] Elsewhere, in a comment of lavatorial crudity, Shadwell is the object of ridicule: 'loads of Sh - - almost choakt the way,' says Dryden.[10]

Behind the abuse was the contentious question of modes of comedy used in Restoration theatre. To Shadwell, a man disposed to coarseness, the comedies of sophisticated wit which Dryden championed had little purpose other than to 'delight the fancy onely'. Rather, the playwright's honest duty was 'to reprehend the Vices and Follies of the Age',[11] a cause that led Shadwell as if along a 'seventeenth-century thoroughfare'[12] amid what he called 'the common conversation of the World',[13] where the imperfections of his characters authenticate their shared humanity. His purpose was to create a comedy of 'humours' in imitation of Ben Jonson whose plays like *Volpone* and *Every Man in his Humour* he admired for what he called their 'perfect Representations of Human Life'.[14] For Jonson it is the balance – or imbalance – of the four mediaeval humours (or elements) of fire, air, water and earth that determines temperament[15] and which Shadwell's characters are likewise powerless to change; he sees to it that man does not escape the folly of his ruling passions:

> A Humor is the Byas of the Mind,
> By which with violence 'tis one way inclin'd:
> It makes our Actions lean on one side still,
> And in all Changes that way bends the Will.[16]

Shadwell was happy to see unmasked what William Wycherley in *The Gentleman Dancing Master* (1672) called 'this masquerading age'. The wearing of vizards and 'strange antick masking habits'[17] at metropolitan revels, theatres and in the parks was a fashion which added to an air of foppish excess. 'I am never in my element but when I am adventuring about an Intriguo, or Masquerading about business,' explains a coxcomb, Sir Samuel Hearty, in Shadwell's *The Virtuoso* (1676). 'Now you shall see me shew my parts.' When 'whores pass[ed] for ladies, fops for wits and rakes for heroes'[18] in an enticing confusion of identities, duplicitous garb became the badge of moral ambiguity: 'Whatever extravagances we commit in these faces,' admit two masquers, 'our own may not be obliged to answer 'em.'[19] And even wit itself grew degenerate. This prized 'quickness of apprehension'[20]was, in the 'spongy brain[s]' of its pretenders, mere raillery, ridicule or detraction. [21]

Prologue to *The Virtuoso*

You came with such an eager appetite
To a late Play, which gave so great delight;
Our Poet fears, that by so rich a Treat,
Your Palates are become too delicate.
Yet since y'have had Rhime for a relishing Bit,
To give a better taste to Comick Wit.
But this requires expence of time and pains,
Too great, alas, for Poets' slender gains.
For Wit, like *China,* should long buried lie,
Before it ripens to good Comedy;
A thing we ne'r have seen since *Jonson's* days,
And but a few of his were perfect Plays.
Now Drudges of the Stage must oft appear,
They must be bound to scribble twice a year.
Thus the thin thred-bare Vicar still must toil,
Whilst the fat lazie Doctor bears the spoil.
In the last Comedy some Wits were shown;
In this are fools that much infest the Town.
Plenty of fops, grievances of the Age,
Whose nauseous Figures ne'r were on a Stage.
He cannot say they'll please you, but they're new;
And he hopes you will say h' has drawn 'em true.
He's sure in Wit he cann't excel the rest,
He'd but be thought to write a Fool the best.
Such Fools as haunt and trouble Men of Wit,
And spight of them will for their Pictures sit.
Yet no one Coxcomb in this Play is shown,
No one Man's humour makes a part alone,
But scatter'd follies gather'd into one.
He says, if with new Fops he can but please,
He'll twice a year produce as new as these.

Ben Jonson's patron, William Cavendish, Duke of Newcastle, was Shadwell's too. 'I have been more obliged by my Lord Duke than by any Man', he acknowledges in the dedication to *The Humorists* (1671) which is addressed to 'the most Illustrious' Princess Margaret, the Duke's wife.[22] Shadwell assures her 'that the Interest of all Poets is to fly for protection to Welbecke [House]; which will never fail to be their Sanctuary, so long as there you are pleased so nobly to patronize Poesie, and so happily practise it.'[23]Elsewhere, Shadwell does not spare a fawning gravity. He has received 'unwearied Bounty' which gratitude 'will not suffer me to smother...in silence.'[24]Newcastle's name, he says, 'will be Eternaliz'd in this Nation, for your Wit beyond all Poets; Judgment and Prudence, before all Statesmen; ...Virtue and Temperance, above all Philosophers' (*The Libertine*, 1676); his dedicatee is 'the only Maecenas of our Age' (*Epsom-Wells*, 1672).[25]

To be the recipient of patronage in seventeenth-century England gave no shelter from the vilifying voices of either literary or political detractors. Shadwell had attracted rancour when he firmly aligned himself with Shaftesbury's Whig party, who were seeking to disable Charles II's (Catholic) brother James from inheriting the throne in favour of the Protestant Duke of Monmouth – to whom the dramatist had dedicated his opera *Psyche*. Furthermore, with distrust of Catholics running high in the years following Thomas Pickering's so-called 'Popish Plot' to assassinate Charles in August 1678, Shadwell had to accept, from the Master of the Revels, cuts in the text of *The Lancashire Witches* (1681) because 'several profest Papists' believed he had written a satire upon the Church of England. Another clamorous party spoke of sedition and treason – that 'the Scope of the Play was against the Government of England'.[26] The censored version lived, however, despite the best efforts of a party of hissers at its performances.

When Dryden, an arch-Tory, published an attack on Shaftesbury, *The Medal, A Satire Against Sedition*, Shadwell showed that he could return hostility in good measure. In his vituperative reply, *The Medal of John Bayes, A Satyr against Folly and Knavery* (1682), the Tory spirit 'seems...to breathe forth nothing but Ruine, Murther, and Massacre'. Dryden himself 'is now become so infamous, that his Libels will be thought Panegyricks.'[27]

The political tide, however, soon cast Shadwell upon a bleak shore. For more than seven years, during which he withdrew entirely from controversy, theatres shunned his work. In the prologue to *Bury-Fair* (1689), Shadwell wrote of having been 'silenc'd for a Non-conformist Poet'. Another patron, the dramatist and wit Sir Charles Sedley – 'whom I have heard speak more Wit at a Supper, than all my Adversaries, with their Heads joyn'd together, can write in a year'[28] – stood by him with gifts of money.

When yet another patron, Charles Sackville, Earl of Dorset and Middlesex, became William's and Mary's Lord Chamberlain following the Bloodless Revolution of 1688, he recommended Shadwell for the post of Poet Laureate, in which he succeeded his adversary, Dryden. 'I will not pretend to determine how great a poet Shadwell is,' explained the Earl, 'but I am sure that he is an honest man.' Shadwell is the only Norfolk man to have held the post which (for the last time) was coupled with that of Historiographer Royal.[29] The statutory £300 and 'One Butt or Pipe of the best Canary wine' paid annually was welcome reward for the man Dryden had earlier described as 'liquor'd every chink.'[30]

As well as offering official panegyrics in honour of the Revolution, the new Laureate heaped praise upon the sovereign in, for example, *An Ode on the Queen's Birth-Day, Sang before their Majesties at Whitehal[l]* (1689), set to music by Purcell. Two tributes appeared in 1690: *Ode on the Anniversary of the King's Birth* and, following the Battle of the Boyne from which the exiled King James fled the field, *Ode to the King, On His Return from Ireland*. Shadwell's *A Song for St Cecilia's Day, 1690* (with music by Robert King) was, in all likelihood, performed 'by the best Voices and Hands in Town'[31] at Stationers' Hall – as was the yearly custom.

A Song for St Cecilia's Day, 1690

O Sacred Harmony, prepare our Lays,
While on *Cecilia's* Day, we sing your Praise,
From Earth to Heav'n our warbling Voices raise!

II

Join all ye glorious Instruments around,
The yielding Air with your Vibrations wound,
And fill Heav'n's Conclave with the mighty Sound.

III

You did at first the warring Atoms join,
Made Qualities most opposite combine,
While Discords did with pleasing Concords twine.

IV

The Universe you fram'd, you still sustain;
Without you what in Tune does now remain
Wou'd jangle into *Chaos* once again.

V

It does your most transcendent Glory prove,
That, to compleat immortal Joys above,
There must be Harmony to crown their Love.

VI

Dirges with Sorrow still inspire
The doleful and lamenting Quire,
With swelling Hearts and flowing Eyes,
They solemnize their Obsequies;
For Grief they frequent Discords chuse,
Long Bindings and Chromaticks use.
Organs and Viols sadly Groan
To the Voice's dismal Tone.

VII

If Love's gentle Passions we
Express, there must be Harmony;
We touch the soft and tender Flute,
The sprinkling and melodious Lute,
When we describe the tickling Smart
Which does invade a Love-sick Heart:
Sweet Nymphs in pretty Murmurs plain,
All chill and panting with the pleasing Pain,
Which can be eas'd by nothing but the Swain.

VIII

If Poets, in a lofty Epic Strain,
Some ancient-noble History recite,
How Heroes love, and puissant Conquerors fight,
Or how on cruel Fortune they complain:
Or if Muse the Fate of Empires sings,
The Change of Crowns, the Rise and Fall of Kings:

CHORUS
'Tis sacred Musick does impart
Life and Vigour to the Art;
It makes the dumb-Poetic Pictures breath,
Victor's and Poet's Names it saves from Death.

IX
How does the thund'ring Martial Song
Provoke the Military Throng!
The Haut-boys and the warlike Fife,
. With Clamors of the Deaf'ning Drum,
Make Peasants bravely hazard Life,
And quicken those whom Fears benum!
The Clangor of the Trumpet's Sound
Fills all the dusty Place around
And does from neighb'ring Hills rebound:
Io triumph when we sing,
We make the trembling Valleys ring.

Grand CHORUS
All Instruments and Voices fit the Quire,
While we enchanting Harmony admire.
What mighty Wonders by our Art are taught,
What Miracles by sacred Numbers wrought
On Earth: In Heav'n, no Joys are perfect found,
'Till by Celestial Harmony they're crown'd.

Most of Shadwell's dramatic poetry is found in prologues and epilogues (thirty-six in number) which expose the shifting play in the relations between the Restoration dramatist and his audience. Represented by the speaker, he addresses a fickle playhouse public as quick to ambush success as to grant fleeting applause.[32] 'Let me the proudest of the Hissers see,' he demands in *The Amorous Bigotte* (1690), and 'I'll make him know he is no match for me.' Within the plays appear a number of songs often incidental to the plot: a tavern song, for example, in *A True Widow* (1678); an erotic one in *The Libertine* (1675). In the near-silent period before his last plays came to the stage in the benign laureate years of William's and Mary's reign, Shadwell published (in 1687) a translation with notes of *The Tenth Satyr of Juvenal*.

A corpulent Thomas Shadwell, long troubled with gout, died of a medicinal overdose of opium on 19th or 20th November 1692. At his request, he was buried 'in Flannel with the least charge that may bee.'

William Cowper 1731-1800

Oh! for a closer walk with God,
A Calm and heav'nly frame;
A light to shine upon the road
That leads me to the Lamb!

William Cowper found peace of mind elusive. Before a third major depression in 1773 he confided to John Newton, the Evangelical preacher with whom he was collaborating in writing *Olney Hymns*: 'The Lord, I trust, will give peace of mind in his own time; but I can truly say for the most part that my soul is among lions'.[1] Rather than discern a 'smiling' providence in the affairs of daily life, he was liable to perceive within the shadows some contrary intent. In time, a sense of being excluded from God's mercy was complete. He claimed he was 'Damn'd below Judas'.[2]

A pattern of tormented schooldays, and the death of his mother Ann two days before his sixth birthday had lost him his nerve. He fell prey to fears real and imagined, and was forever searching for 'the thorn beneath every rose'.[3] In adult life the frightened boy remained trapped in the heart of the man.

By nature passive, Cowper granted undue influence to the inner world of his dreams. Rarely did they bring him delight, as when, in 1764, he attributed the lifting of a long period of despair to the tender dream of a boy 'just out of leading reins', who danced up to his bedside with a self-reliance that might have been Cowper's had his childhood been less blighted.

The dream, in conjunction with a chance reading from the Epistle to the Romans concerning the sufficiency of Christ's atonement for sin, prompted not only immediate recovery, but his conversion to Evangelical faith. Dr Nathaniel Cotton, who at the time was caring for Cowper in his private asylum, the Collegium Insanorum at St Albans, feared 'lest the sudden transition from despair to joy should terminate in frenzy'. But intense religious feeling, an Evangelical's 'test of growth in grace',[4] had brought temporary assurance of redemption. 'The name of Jesu was like honey and milk upon my tongue and the very sound of it was sufficient to sustain...me'.[5]

The new convert moved to lodgings in Huntingdon on his return to fair health in 1765, to discover that religious ardour cannot be fanned alone. He met the Reverend Morley Unwin and his wife Mary, and soon joined the household as a boarder. Theirs was a homely outpost of salvation[6] where he enjoyed spiritual fellowship in abundance. In Mary, from whose company he was not to be parted until her death some thirty years later, he found a surrogate mother of 'uncommon understanding'[7] and unfailing emotional resources. At Orchard Side in Newton's parish of Olney (in Buckinghamshire), their home after Morley's death (in 1767), they were free to perfect their creed of domestic piety: genteel society had lost all attraction.

Light Shining Out Of Darkness

Newton's Olney hymnbook met the needs of fervent congregations no longer at ease with the tradition of metrical psalm-singing. It was to run to thirty-seven editions before 1863. Cowper's hymns (67 in number) are born of an openness to God's way with him: they

William Cowper

speak of strong assurance ('But a prayer-hearing, answering God/Supports me under every load'),[8] and of vulnerability also ('Repair me now, for now mine end doth haste').[9]

Whenever Cowper recollects the sea he cannot do so without emotion. He knew it first on childhood holidays with his mother, at Happisburgh in North Norfolk, where he stayed with an uncle who was curate there. He brooded upon it under the shadow of a final despair on frequent visits to Mundesley in 1798. 'In all its various forms', he wrote, 'it is an object of all others the most suited to affect us with lasting impressions of the awful power that created and controls it'.[10] In his Olney hymns God is both the author and subduer of storms. 'O Lord, the pilot's part perform', he pleads, 'and guide me thro' the storm'.[11] Cowper fears that, without the 'chastisement' he believes God metes out to him to make him worthy of salvation, he will become a castaway abandoned without understanding of God's mysterious ways.

> God moves in a mysterious way,
>   His wonders to perform;
> He plants his footsteps in the sea,
>   And rides upon the storm.
>
> Deep in unfathomable mines
>   Of never failing skill,
> He treasures up his bright designs,
>   And works his sov'reign will.

Ye fearful saints, fresh courage take;
The clouds ye so much dread
Are big with mercy, and shall break
In blessings on your head.

Judge not the Lord by feeble sense
But trust him for his grace;
Behind a frowning providence
He hides a smiling face.

His purposes will ripen fast,
Unfolding every hour;
The bud may have a bitter taste,
But sweet will be the flower.

Blind unbelief is sure to err,
And scan his work in vain:
God is his own interpreter,
And he will make it plain.

The years at Olney – and at nearby Weston Underwood from 1786 – were a fertile period for Cowper. The moral satires published in *Poems* (1782) ventured beyond eighteenth-century precedents to explore the human condition before God from a standpoint of convinced belief. The first of them, 'The Progress of Error' is notably uncompromising:

I am no preacher, let this hint suffice,
The cross once seen, is death to ev'ry vice;
Else he that hung there, suffer'd all his pain,
Bled, groan'd, and agoniz'd, and died in vain.[12]

The long autobiographical work, *The Task* (1785), in which he seeks to justify his choice of life and to understand its ambivalences, became the most widely read text in England until the turn of the century; its inspiration was Milton in his blindness discoursing on inner light.[13] And after he was told of a draper whose horse ran away with him, he wrote 'John Gilpin', the most popular of his poems.

On the Receipt of My Mother's Picture Out of Norfolk

'I kissed it, and hung it where it is the last object that I see at night, and, of course, the first on which I open my eyes in the morning'.[14] The miniature of his mother Ann (Donne), painted on copper by Heins, came to Cowper as a gift from his Norfolk cousin, Anne Bodham, in February 1790. She wears a gown of blue, trimmed with braid of gold and pearls, and looks out with large dark eyes and gentle expression. The artist has captured a delicate frailty. William was the only one of her six children to survive beyond the age of two, and so became the sole recipient of her poignant tenderness. No week passed without remembrance of her.

Recalling her death, Cowper juxtaposes contrary destinies: his mother, 'as a gallant bark', comes safely to the heavenly harbour on the tide of God's redeeming love; her son, adrift and without compass, is subject to perverse elements bent upon setting him 'more distant from a prosp'rous course'.

O that those lips had language! Life has pass'd
With me but roughly since I heard thee last.
Those lips are thine - thy own sweet smile I see,
The same, that oft in childhood solac'd me;
Voice only fails, else how distinct they say,
'Grieve not, my child, chase all thy fears away!'
The meek intelligence of those dear eyes
(Blest be the art that can immortalize,
The art that baffles Time's tyrannic claim
To quench it) here shines on me still the same.

Faithful remembrancer of one so dear,
O welcome guest, though unexpected here!
Who bidd'st me honour with an artless song,
Affectionate, a mother lost so long.
I will obey, not willingly alone,
But gladly, as the precept were her own:
And, while that face renews my filial grief,
Shall steep me in Elysian reverie,
A momentary dream, that thou art she.

My mother! when I learn'd that thou wast dead,
Say, wast thou conscious of the tears I shed?
Hover'd thy spirit o'er thy sorr'wing son,
Wretch even then, life's journey just begun?
Perhaps thou gav'st me, though unfelt, a kiss;
Perhaps a tear, if souls can weep in bliss -
Ah that maternal smile! it answers - Yes.
I heard the bell toll'd on thy burial day,
I saw the hearse, that bore thee slow away,
And, turning from my nurs'ry window, drew
A long, long sigh, and wept a last adieu!
But was it such? - It was - Where thou art gone
Adieus and farewells are a sound unknown.
May I but meet thee on that perfect shore,
The parting word shall pass my lips no more!
Thy maidens, griev'd themselves at my concern,
Oft gave me promise of thy quick return.
What ardently I wish'd, I long believ'd,
And, disappointed still, was still deceiv'd.
By expectation ev'ry day beguil'd
Dupe of to-morrow even from a child.
Thus many a sad to-morrow came and went,
Till, all my stock of infant sorrow spent,
I learn'd at last submission to my lot,
But, though I less deplor'd thee, ne'er forgot.

Where once we dwelt our name is heard no more,
Children not thine have trod my nurs'ry floor;

And where the gard'ner Robin, day be day,
Drew me to school along the public way,
Delighted with my bauble coach, and wrapp'd
In scarlet mantle warm, and velvet cap,
'Tis now become a hist'ry little known,
That once we call'd the past'ral house our own.
Shortliv'd possession! but the record fair,
That mem'ry keeps of all thy kindness there,
Still outlives many a storm, that has effac'd
A thousand other themes less deeply trac'd.
Thy nightly visits to my chamber made,
That thou mightst know me safe and warmly laid;
Thy morning bounties ere I left my home,
The biscuit, or confectionary plum;
The fragrant waters on my cheeks bestow'd
By thy own hand, till fresh they shone and glow'd;
All this, and more endearing still than all,
Thy constant flow of love, that knew no fall,
Ne'er roughen'd by those cataracts and breaks,
That humour interpos'd too often makes;
All this still legible in mem'ry's page,
And still to be so to my latest age,
Adds joy to duty, makes me glad to pay
Such honours to thee as my numbers may;
Perhaps a frail memorial, but sincere,
Not scorn'd in Heav'n, though little notic'd here.

Could Time, his flight revers'd, restore the hours,
When, playing with thy vesture's tissu'd flow'rs,
The violet, the pink, and jessamine,
I prick'd them into paper with a pin,
(And thou wast happier than myself the while,
Wouldst softly speak, and stroke my head, and smile)
Could those few pleasant days again appear,
Might one wish bring them, would I wish them here?
I would not trust my heart – the dear delight
Seems so to be desir'd, perhaps I might. –
But no – what here we call our life is such,
So little to be lov'd, and thou so much,
That I should ill requite thee to constrain
Thy unbound spirit into bonds again.

Thou, as a gallant bark from Albion's coast
(The storms all weather'd and the ocean cross'd)
Shoots into port at some well-haven'd isle,
Where spices breathe, and brighter seasons smile,
There sits quiescent on the floods, that show
Her beauteous form reflected clear below,

While airs impregnated with incense play
Around her, fanning light her streamers gay;
So thou, with sails how swift! hast reach'd the shore,
'Where tempests never beat nor billows roar,'
And thy lov'd consort on the dang'rous tide
Of life long since has anchor'd by thy side.
But me, scarce hoping to attain that rest,
Always from port withheld, always distress'd –
Me howling blasts drive devious, tempest-toss'd,
Sails ripp'd, seams op'ning wide, and compass lost,
And day by day some current's thwarting force
Sets me more distant from a prosp'rous course.
Yet O the thought, that thou art safe, and he!
That thought is joy, arrive what may to me.
My boast is not, that I deduce my birth
From loins enthron'd, and rulers of the Earth;
But higher far my proud pretensions rise –
The son of parents pass'd into the skies.
And now, farewell – Time unrevok'd has run
His wonted course, yet what I wish'd is done.
By contemplation's help, not sought in vain,
I seem t'have liv'd my childhood o'er again;
To have renew'd the joys that once were mine,
Without the sin of violating thine;
And, while the wings of Fancy still are free,
And I can view this mimic show of thee,
Time has but half succeeded in his theft –
Thyself remov'd, thy pow'r to soothe me left.

It was an unforeseen visit by Cowper's second cousin, John Johnson, which re-established contact with his Donne relations in Norfolk. The young 'Johnny of Norfolk', as Cowper called him, was given to cultivate ambitious social connections, and wished to bask in an association with the distinguished poet. A year earlier he had made himself known even to Charles Howard, eleventh Duke of Norfolk, after the Donne line had been traced back to the first Duke by the editor of the Paston letters, Sir John Fenn. Johnny celebrated the family seat at Audley End, near Saffron Walden, in a poem of his own, written at the Duke's suggestion. A poor versifier himself, he now showed it to Cowper, passing it off as the work of the Duke. He revealed the lie only when Cowper was openly critical.[15]

The elder cousin was forgiving. He saw in Johnny qualities he liked to think a son of his own would have come to possess: engaging ingenuity, a reflective mind, and 'an understanding that, in due time, will know how to show itself to advantage'.[16] Soon, with Cowper's active encouragement, he was seeking ordination. For his part, Johnny gave near filial devotion. When Mrs Unwin suffered a third stroke in April 1794, Cowper's mental health began to deteriorate and, by the summer of the following year, Johnny offered to move them both to his house in Dereham where he held the curacy.[17]

When Cowper refused to face the prospect of living in the centre of a busy market town, an aunt, Harriet Balls, rented the parsonage at North Tuddenham for a few summer weeks before the arrival of the new incumbent in August 1795. Johnny then took the invalids to Mundesley, to lodge with a German apothecary, Dr Kaliere, whose house overlooked the sea. In spite of the inconvenience, Johnny travelled the forty miles each weekend to take services in Dereham while Cowper fretted for his return. By the time Cowper had become reconciled to living at Johnny's house in Dereham and had moved there (in October 1796 after an unhappy residence at Dunham Lodge near Swaffham), he was ready to accompany Johnny home after their frequent visits to the coast.

'My chamber commands a very near view of the ocean', Cowper records, 'and the ships at high water approach the coast so closely that a man furnished with better eyes than mine might, I doubt not, discern the sailors from the window'.[18] He writes of walking the coast for eight miles a day, his face sheltered by an umbrella from the blowing sands. Johnny's diary for 1798 describes an encounter while out in a rowing boat when the master of a wine ship from Oporto invited the party to go aboard. But knowing Cowper's 'fearful forebodings' about meeting anyone outside his close circle, Johnny declined the offer. Cowper 'observed that he had missed the only chance he should ever have of tasting *real* port wine'.[19]

Inevitably, a sense of regret predominates: 'Alas!' he writes from Mundesley, 'I tread a shore within [sight]...of a place where I passed some of the happiest days of my youth, in company with those whom I loved and by whom I *was* beloved. That pleasure I must know no more'.[20]

The Cast-Away

Within the routines of the Dereham curacy Johnny and Catherine (his wife) maintained patient vigil over Cowper's troubled mind. For long periods he had remained afloat on tides of intense, but unsustainable, religious feeling. Now, spiritual accidie was all but smothering interest in life itself. Even the pleasures of the natural world seemed barren. At 'a time of affliction' he admitted: nature's 'animating smile withdrawn,/ has lost its beauties and its pow'rs'.[21]

After he left Mary Unwin's deathbed (on 17th December 1796) - exclaiming 'Oh God - was it for this?' - any show of grief was confined to his saturnine silences: he was not heard to make mention of her again. The voices that for some years had troubled his dreams now began to hound his days. By way of distraction, he allowed Johnny to read to him, sometimes from the recently published ninth edition of his verse. And, fitfully, he was able to complete revisions of his translations of Homer, begun in 1784.

The predicament of a sailor 'canted overboard' off Cape Horn, as recounted in Richard Walter's *A Voyage Round the World* by... *George Anson, 1748,* inspired 'The Cast-Away', Cowper's last, and finest, lyric poem. 'We were the more grieved at his unhappy fate, since we lost sight of him struggling with the waves,' wrote Walter, '...and conceived from the manner in which he swam, that he might continue sensible for a considerable time longer, of the horror attending his irretrievable situation.'[22]Cowper, likewise attended by terrors – that spoke to him of damnation – seemed cast beyond the powers of friends to help. 'We perish'd, each alone,' he writes in the final stanza – poet and sailor lost to analogous fates.

William Cowper died on 25th April 1800, and was buried in St Edmund's chapel within the north transept of Dereham Church.

Obscurest night involv'd the sky,
    Th' Atlantic billows roar'd,
When such a destin'd wretch as I
    Wash'd headlong from on board,
Of friends, of hope, of all bereft,
His floating home for ever left.

No braver chief could Albion boast
    Than he with whom he went,
Nor ever ship left Albion's coast
    With warmer wishes sent.
He lov'd them both, but both in vain,
Nor him beheld, nor her again.

Not long beneath the whelming brine
    Expert to swim, he lay;
Nor soon he felt his strength decline
    Or courage die away;
But wag'd with death a lasting strife
Ssupported by despair of life.

He shouted: nor his friends had fail'd
    To check the vessel's course,
But so the furious blast prevail'd
    That, pitiless perforce,
They left their outcast mate behind,
And scudded still before the wind.

Some succour yet they could afford;
    And, such as storms allow,
The cask, the coop, the floated cord
    Delay'd not to bestow.
But he, they knew, nor ship nor shore,
Whate'er they gave, should visit more.

Nor, cruel as it seem'd, could he
    Their haste, himself, condemn,
Aware that flight in such a sea
    Alone could rescue *them;*
Yet bitter felt it still to die
Deserted, and his friends so nigh.

He long survives who lives an hour
    In ocean, self-upheld:
And so long he with unspent pow'r
    His destiny repell'd:
And ever as the minutes flew,
Entreated help, or cried – 'Adieu!'

At length, his transient respite past,
    His comrades, who before
Had heard his voice in ev'ry blast,
    Could catch the sound no more:
For then, by toil subdued, he drank
The stifling wave, and then he sank.

No poet wept him, but the page
    Of narrative sincere
That tells his name, his worth, his age,
    Is wet with Anson's tear;
And tears by bards or heroes shed
Alike immortalize the dead.

I, therefore, purpose not or dream,
    Descanting on his fate,
To give the melancholy theme
    A more enduring date;
But mis'ry still delights to trace
Its semblance in another's case.

No voice divine the storm allay'd,
    No light propitious shone;
When, snatch'd from all effectual aid,
    We perish'd, each alone;
But I, beneath a rougher sea,
    And whelm'd in deeper gulfs than he.

Thomas Hood 1799-1845

Two years before Thomas Carlyle (in *Chartism*, 1845) referred, with seminal effect, to the social problems of the labouring poor as 'the Condition of England Question', Thomas Hood had etched the plight of a London seamstress upon the metropolitan conscience.

He was moved to compose the humanitarian verses, 'The Song of the Shirt' on hearing how the widow, Biddell, in wishing to provide her two children with dry bread, had pawned articles belonging to her employer. She had informed the Lambeth Police Court that for the wage of seven shillings a week – the sum her foreman adjudged to be a 'good living', and from which she had to supply her own needles and thread – she was required to work ninety-six hours. *The Times* averred that the widow was from 'every moral point of view, as much a slave as any negro who ever toiled under as cruel taskmasters in the West Indies'.[1] Spared a term in a house of correction, she was sent to the workhouse.

Hood had touched a chord: 'The Song of the Shirt' was hawked on ballad sheets and woven into handkerchiefs; it was read, even from pulpits. Illiterates learnt it by heart and rude adaptations were heard about the streets.[2]

For the majority, the early years of Victoria's reign (1837-42) were doleful ones. Widening inequalities (brought about by falling incomes in a severe depression), provoked a number of 'social' novels, of which Hood's further public poems were the precursors. His *A Drop of Gin* (1843), *The Pauper's Christmas Carol* (1843), and the compelling *The Bridge of Sighs* (1844) – London's Waterloo Bridge so favoured by suicides – were soon followed by Disraeli's *Sybil, or The Two Nations* (1845), Elizabeth Gaskell's *Mary Barton* (1848), and Charles Kingsley's *Yeast* (1848). When the 'hungry 'forties' had run their

course, Hood's fellow Londoner, Dickens, whose shared vision informs their correspondence, and the reviews Hood wrote for magazines, depicted, in *Hard Times* (1854),
the 'fictional Gehenna' he called Coketown.[3]

Hood possessed an innate optimism which near-chronic invalidism quite failed to tame.
'The raven croaked,' he said, 'but I persuaded myself that it was the nightingale. There was
the smell of mould, but I remembered that it nourished the violets.'[4] Thus he bore lung
diseases and liver complaints, the concomitants of rheumatic heart disease, with 'smiling
heroism'.[5] And adding to his troubles were pecuniary difficulties not always of his own
making. 'I have to be a lively Hood for a livelihood', he famously punned, and thereby
acknowledged a gift for comic verse which often received churlish approval from friends,
but secured for his devoted wife, Jane, and their four daughters, the semblance of a stable
income.

With the publication of the popular *Whims and Oddities*, exuberant punning became
synonymous with Hood's name:

> Ben Battle was a soldier bold,
>   And used to war's alarms;
> But a cannon-ball took off his legs,
>   So he laid down his arms!
>
> Now as they bore him off the field,
>   Said he, 'Let others shoot,
> For here I leave my second leg,
>   And the Forty-second Foot!'
>   (Faithless Nelly Gray, ll. 1-8)

The comic annuals Hood published from 1830 to 1839 and later reissued in shilling
parts called *Hood's Own*, provided entertainment for the rising middle class. 'To make
laugh is my calling,' he said, yet when he laid aside the mantle of comedy and spoke (as
Thackeray recorded) 'out of his heart, all England and America listened with tears and
wonder.' To pun was to deflect the pricking of a sensitive moral conscience.

The Dream of Eugene Aram, the Murderer

In a derivative poem, 'Ode to Autumn', Hood personifies Keats's benign season of
'mellow fruitfulness' as a female figure who wears 'a face of care'. His season is a truly
sombre one with 'Enough of fear and shadowy despair,/To frame her cloudy prison for the
soul!' He knows too well the world of anguish and pain so that, as the critic John Heath-
Stubbs has suggested, he has allowed the shades of melancholy to press upon him 'in
excess of the actual emotions which would be excited by the theme.'[6] And as were many of
his more fortunate contemporaries, the sickly poet was yet further drawn to the twilight
world of Gothic melodrama and to the grim regions of the macabre and the grotesque.

The story of Eugene Aram (1704-1759) provided Hood with a gruesome panorama.
When the body of the executed murderer-schoolmaster from King's Lynn was hung in
chains from Knaresborough Castle, it was told how his wife would stand watch to pick up
his bones as they dropped; further, his children would take strangers to view the body.

Aram's crime was the murder of one Daniel Clark in revenge for his wife's infidelity
with him. He had left Knaresborough hastily (in 1745) on suspicion of having been Clark's

accomplice in a matter of fraud. He was arrested some thirteen years later while serving on the staff of the Corporation School of Lynn Regis; a skeleton had been found in a cave near Knaresborough. Aram was convicted and executed on 6th August 1759, having failed to take his own life by opening his veins with a razor.

Driven by uncontrollable remorse, the Aram of Hood's poem couches his confession in the form of a dream which he recounts to a schoolboy he discovers reading Gessner's *The Death of Abel*. In the shadow of Cain, the boy listens in bewildered fear to the disclosure of a tortured mind. Aram, for his part, shares nightmare reality with one 'untouched by sin', a lad as once he was, and innocent of what Thomas Gray (in 'Ode on a Distant Prospect of Eton College') acknowledges as being 'The ministers of human fate,/And black Misfortune's baleful train!'[7]

> 'Twas in the prime of summer time,
>   An evening calm and cool,
> And four-and-twenty happy boys
>   Came bounding out of school:
> There were some that ran and some that leapt,
>   Like troutlets in a pool.
>
> Away they sped with gamesome minds,
>   And souls untouched by sin;
> To a level mead they came, and there
>   They drave the wickets in:
> Pleasantly shown the setting sun
>   Over the town of Lynn.
>
> Like sportive deer they coursed about,
>   And shouted as they ran, –
> Turning to mirth all things of earth,
>   As only boyhood can;
> But the Usher sat remote from all,
>   A melancholy man!
>
> His hat was off, his vest apart,
>   To catch heaven's blessed breeze;
> For a burning thought was in his brow,
>   And his bosom ill at ease:
> So he leaned his head on his hands, and read
>   The book upon his knees!
>
> Leaf after leaf he turned it o'er,
>   Nor ever glanced aside,
> For the peace of his soul he read that book
>   In the golden eventide:
> Much study had made him very lean,
>   And pale, and leaden-eyed.

At last he shut the pond'rous tome,
  With a fast and fervent grasp
He strained the dusky covers close,
  And fixed the brazen hasp:
'Oh, God! could I so close my mind,
  And clasp it with a clasp!'

Then leaping on his feet upright,
  Some moody turns he took, –
Now up the mead, then down the mead,
  And past a shady nook, –
And lo! he saw a little boy
  That pored upon a book.

'My gentle lad, what is't you read –
  Romance or fairy fable?
Or is it some historic page,
  Of kings and crowns unstable?'
The young boy gave an upward glance, –
  'It is *The Death of Abel.*'

The Usher took six hasty strides,
  As smit with sudden pain, –
Six hasty strides beyond the place,
  Then slowly back again;
And down he sat beside the lad,
  And talked with him of Cain;

And, long since then, of bloody men,
  Whose deeds tradition saves;
Of lonely folk cut off unseen,
  And hid in sudden graves;
Of horrid stabs, in groves forlorn,
  And murders done in caves;

And how the sprites of injured men
  Shriek upward from the sod, –
Ay, how the ghostly hand will point
  To show the burial clod;
And unknown facts of guilty acts
  Are seen in dreams from God!

He told how murderers walk the earth
  Beneath the curse of Cain, –
With crimson clouds before their eyes,
  And flames about their brain:
For blood has left upon their souls
  Its everlasting stain!

'And well,' quoth he, 'I know for truth,
  Their pangs must be extreme, –
Woe, woe, unutterable woe, –
  Who spill life's sacred stream!
For why? Methought, last night, I wrought
  A murder, in a dream!

'One that had never done me wrong –
  A feeble man and old;
I led him to a lonely field,
  The moon shone clear and cold:
Now here, said I, this man shall die,
  And I will have his gold!

'Two sudden blows with a ragged stick,
  And one with a heavy stone,
One hurried gash with a hasty knife, –
  And then the deed was done:
There was nothing lying at my foot
  But lifeless flesh and bone!

'Nothing but lifeless flesh and bone,
  That could not do me ill;
And yet I feared him all the more,
  For lying there so still:
There was a manhood in his look,
  That murder could not kill!

'And lo! the universal air
  Seemed lit with ghastly flame;
Ten thousand thousand dreadful eyes
  Were looking down in blame:
I took the dead man by the hand,
  And called upon his name!

'Oh God! it made me quake to see
  Such sense within the slain!
But when I touched the lifeless clay,
  The blood gushed out amain!
For every clot, a burning spot
  Was scorching in my brain!

'My head was like an ardent coal,
  My heart as solid ice;
My wretched, wretched soul, I knew,
  Was at the Devil's price:
A dozen times I groaned; the dead
  Had never groaned but twice!

'And now, from forth the frowning sky,
  From the Heaven's topmost height,
I heard a voice – the awful voice
  Of the blood-avenging sprite –
"Thou guilty man! take up thy dead
  And hide it from my sight!"

'I took the dreary body up,
  And cast it in a stream, –
A sluggish water, black as ink,
  The depth was so extreme:
My gentle Boy, remember this
  Is nothing but a dream!

'Down went the corse with a hollow plunge,
  And vanished in the pool;
Anon I cleansed my bloody hands,
  And washed my forehead cool,
And sat among the urchin young,
  That evening in the school.

'Oh, Heaven! to think of their white souls,
  And mine so black and grim!
I could not share in childish prayer,
  Nor join in Evening Hymn:
Like a Devil of the Pit I seemed,
  'Mid holy Cherubim!

'And peace went with them, one and all,
  And each calm pillow spread;
But guilt was my grim Chamberlain
  That lighted me to bed;
And drew my midnight curtains round,
  With fingers bloody red!

'All night I lay in agony,
  In anguish dark and deep,
My fevered eyes I dared not close,
  But stared aghast at Sleep:
For Sin had rendered unto her
  The keys of Hell to keep!

'All night I lay in agony,
  From weary chime to chime,
With one besetting horrid hint,
  That racked me all the time;
A mighty yearning, like the first
  Fierce impulse unto crime!

'One stern tyrannic thought, that made
  All other thoughts its slave;
Stronger and stronger every pulse
  Did that temptation crave, –
Still urging me to go and see
  The Dead Man in his grave!

'Heavily I rose up, as soon
  As light was in the sky,
And sought the black accursed pool
  With a wild misgiving eye;
And I saw the Dead in the river bed,
  For the faithless stream was dry.

'Merrily rose the lark, and shook
  The dewdrop from its wing;
But I never marked its morning flight,
  I never heard it sing:
For I was stooping once again
  Under the horrid thing.

'With breathless speed, like a soul in chase,
  I took him up and ran;
There was no time to dig a grave
  Before the day began:
In a lonesome wood, with heaps of leaves,
  I hid the murdered man!

'And all that day I read in school,
  But my thought was otherwhere;
As soon as the midday task was done,
  In secret I was there:
And a mighty wind had swept the leaves,
  And still the corse was bare!

'Then down I cast me on my face,
  And first began to weep,
For I knew my secret then was one
  That earth refused to keep:
Or land or sea, though he should be
  Ten thousand fathoms deep.

'So wills the fierce avenging Sprite,
  Till blood for blood atones!
Ay, though he's buried in a cave,
  And trodden down with stones,
And years have rotted off his flesh, –
  The world shall see his bones!

'Oh God! that horrid, horrid dream
　Besets me now awake!
Again – again, with dizzy brain,
　The human life I take;
And my red right hand grows raging hot,
　Like Cranmer's at the stake.

'And still no peace for the restless clay,
　Will wave or mould allow;
The horrid thing pursues my soul, –
　It stands before me now!'
The fearful Boy looked up, and saw
　Huge drops upon his brow.

That very night, while gentle sleep
　The urchin eyelids kissed,
Two stern-faced men set out from Lynn,
　Through the cold and heavy mist;
And Eugene Aram walked between,
　With gyves upon his wrist.

George Borrow 1803-1881

George Borrow was his father's son. Behind the door of the octagonal summer-house at Oulton Cottage, his home on the Broads near Lowestoft, Borrow hung his father's military uniform and sword, 'the household gods'[1] in whose presence he composed the books which brought the fleeting fame he was to know in his lifetime. Through the impressionable period of his boyhood which spanned twelve years of the Napoleonic Wars, 'home' had been quartering in tent or barracks, as military exigencies determined. His father, Thomas, a recruiting officer with the West Norfolk Militia, and his wife Ann, only briefly enjoyed settled domicile when they lived in the home of Ann's parents at Dumpling Green, close to East Dereham. And it was (probably) here, at the time of the short and precarious Peace of Amiens, that George was conceived.[2] The young Borrow, born to this vagrant rootlessness, was early disposed towards the company of outsiders. '[I have been] here and there, and far and near, going about with soldiers,' he tells his friend, the gypsy Jasper Petulengro in *Lavengro*, the book whose autobiographical vein confirms, as does all his writing from Oulton, 'the traveller's view of things',[3] the detachment which was never to be tested in the crucible of fatherhood.

Thomas Borrow was a pugilist, whose exploits his son cast in the heroic mould. He would tell vividly, for example, of his father's supposed vanquishing (in Hyde Park in 1790) of the soon-to-be champion of England, the bruiser Benjamin Brain, 'whose skin was brown and dusky as that of a toad'. Prowess with fists singled a man out, George Borrow believed, 'amidst hundreds of people with no renown at all, who gaze upon [him] with timid wonder.' Himself a boxing pupil in Norwich of 'the terrible [John] Thurtell', (who was hanged in 1824 for the Gill's Hill Murder of a gambler, William Weare), Borrow attended a number of prize fights, witnessing at the age of seventeen the notable Painter-Oliver bout at North Walsham, when the mighty Cribb was present.[4] Borrow's own triumph over the 'Flaming Tinman', famously described in *Lavengro*, was sealed when he laid upon him a Long Melford (a long right-handed blow) at the fortuitous suggestion of an onlooker; and no doubt he thought those household gods appeased in the proper recording of it.

The Wrestling-Match

As one day I wandered lonely, in extreme distress of mind,
I a pleasant garden entered, hoping comfort there to find.
Up and down I paced the garden till an open space I spied,
There I saw a crowd of people, and I heard a voice that cried:
'Come and see what Love is doing, here is Love performing more
Wondrous feats than e'er were witnessed at Olympian games of yore:
This he conquers, that he conquers, young and old before him lie,
Great and small alike he conquers, none with him a fall must try.'

Hearing this, at once I entered 'midst the crowd collected there,
Some of whom no doubt were eager, like myself, to banish care.
I would fain behold this being, this same wondrous lad survey,
Who, 'twas said, in each encounter bore with ease the prize away.

Quickly I the crowd divided, soon I pierced the multitude,
And this Love stood full before me, and what think you 'twas I view'd?
Why, a boy, a little darling, full of captivating grace,
Rather roguish were his glances, but how lovely was his face!

Soon as I beheld this warrior, gibings I began to throw
At the wretches who had suffered fell defeat from such a foe.
Then, to me his visage turning, of the conquered standing by
One replied, and in replying tears he shed abundantly:
'O, poor youth,' 'twas thus he answered, 'little, little dost thou know
That in coming here thou comest not to joy, but bitter woe.
Tears and pains, and wounds most ghastly, wounds for which there is no cure,
Every kind of evil treatment such as no one can endure.'

When these words I heard him utter I was filled with bitter rage,
And forthwith made preparation with the warrior to engage.
'Harken, Master Love,' I shouted, 'from this spot stir not away,
You and I must have a battle, must engage in deadly fray;
That it may be known for certain which is strongest of us two.'
Then into the arena bounding, there I stood in all men's view,
In the midst of it expecting firm the onset of the foe,
Doubting not, should he attack me, him at once to overthrow.
Love he was not slow to follow with a blythe and joyous air,
Crying out, 'My dearest fellow, for the fight yourself prepare!
Round the waist each other clasping, now let's strive like wrestlers true,
Do your best and I will show you what young Master Love can do.'

Then around the waist I clasped him, he his arms around me wound,
Long we hugged and hugged each other, each his match in t'other found.
Said at length the urchin to me: 'Sadly tired, friend, am I,
Very much fatigued and weary, really, friend, just fit to die.
Therefore take from me, I prythee, what thou anxiously hast sought,
And for which in this arena with me gallantly hast fought.'

Then a blast of wild consuming fire he breathed into my breast,
Straight my breast it quick enkindled, all deprived was I of rest,
Then he ran away exulting to some other wretched wight,
Such a zest he has for conflict, in such fray is his delight.

As for me I fell half senseless on the fatal, fatal spot,
Fierce consuming fire within me, never sure was one so hot.
Rising up, I followed shrieking, 'Oh, have mercy, Love, on me!
See my tears, my sad affliction, cure me of my misery!'

Then he cried, 'Dost not remember all the boasts thy lips out-pour'd?
Know henceforth in every region Love is Conqueror and Lord.'
Thus he cried, and proudly left me, and wherever now I rove,
I reproach myself for thinking I could vanquish mighty Love.

George Borrow

The disbandment of the West Norfolk Militia at the time of Napoleon's exile on Elba brought the Borrows to Norwich from Edinburgh, where the ten-year-old Sassenach had stood his ground through some settled months of schooling, and where he had befriended the regimental drummer-boy and future double-murderer, 'wild Davy' Haggart.[5] Then from Norwich, after a brief introduction to the Grammar School in Upper Close, there was a final uprooting (during Napoleon's Hundred Days), this time to Ireland. This was the country whose language was next, after Romany, to fascinate his ear. Indifferent as he was to much of the regimen prescribed by the Grammar School on his return there as a scholarship boy (in May 1816), he set about acquiring languages by every possible means. With Thomas D'Eterville, an émigré priest, he learned French and Italian, borrowing the while (from the City Library) *The Guide into the Tongues*, which provided 'the Reasons and Derivations of all or the most part of words' in all of nine languages;[6] he talked German with the intemperate and atheist friend of the poet Southey, William Taylor, who welcomed him to the circle of Norwich intellectuals that met regularly at his house at 21 King Street. From Mousha, a Jew, he heard Hebrew,[7] and from an ostler, his native Welsh.[8]

After Borrow had left the Grammar School to be articled to a Norwich solicitor, William Simpson, he received the volume which triggered interest in Continental songs and ballads, in particular those of Scandinavia. Heavy with iron clasps, this book was a collection of Danish ballads published in 1591 by Anders Vedel, a friend of the astronomer Tycho Brahe, and came to him from a country client of Simpson's because he thought Borrow resembled a son lost at sea some years before. Immediately, and with an obsessive single-mindedness, Borrow sought understanding of its language by comparing Dutch and English Bibles. '...I [had] bit my lip until the blood came out; and I occasionally tore a handful from my hair, but that did not mend the matter...' A mere month of relentless employment *did* mend the matter, and he was able to start upon translation.[9]

Romantic Ballads (1826), the fruit of this labour, is a collection of both old Danish *Kiaempe Viser* (Heroic Ballads) and the best of contemporary ones from the works of Oehlenslaeger. Borrow, in the preface, admits of their 'rude...versification', but recommends them as describing 'in vivid and barbaric language scenes of barbaric grandeur which in these days are never witnessed'. A metrical dedication by a friend, Allan Cunningham, accurately echoes Borrow's estimation of them:

> Though rough and rude, those strains are rife
> Of things kin to immortal life,
> Which touch the heart and tinge the cheek,
> As deeply as divinest Greek.

Fewer than two hundred copies were subscribed for in Norwich; the remainder (over three hundred) attracted little interest when they were sent to London.[10] Among subscribers were Bishop Bathurst of Norwich and the painter of vast heroic canvasses, Benjamin Haydon. One man was never to read his copy: John Thurtell was hanged before the book appeared.[11]

Fridleif and Helga
From the Danish of Oehlenslaeger

The woods were in leaf, and they cast a sweet shade;
Among them walk'd Helga, the beautiful maid.

The water is dashing o'er yon little stones;
She sat down beside it, and rested her bones.

She sat down, and soon, from a bush that was near,
Sir Fridleif approach'd her with sword and with spear:

'Ah, pity me, Helga, and fly me not now,
I live, only live, on the smile of thy brow:

'In thy father's whole garden is found not a rose,
Which bright as thyself, and as beautiful grows.'

'Sir Fridleif, thy words are but meant to deceive,
Yet tell me what brings thee so late here at eve.'

'I cannot find rest, and I cannot find ease,
Though sweet sing the linnets among the wild trees;

'If thou wilt but promise, one day to be mine,
No more shall I sorrow, no more shall I pine.'

She sank in his arms, and her cheeks were as red
As the sun when he sinks in his watery bed;

But soon she arose from his loving embrace;
He walk'd by her side, through the wood, for a space.

'Now listen, young Fridleif, the gallant and bold,
Take off from my finger this ring of red gold,

Take off from my finger this ring of red gold,
And part with it not, till in death thou art cold.'

Sir Fridleif stood there in a sorrowful plight,
Salt tears wet his eyeballs, and blinded his sight.

'Go home, and I'll come to thy father with speed,
And claim thee from him, on my mighty grey steed.'

Sir Fridleif, at night, through the thick forest rode,
He fain would arrive at his lov'd one's abode;

His harness was clanking, his helm glitter'd sheen,
His horse was so swift, and himself was so keen:

He reach'd the proud castle, and jump'd on the ground,
His horse to the branch of a linden he bound;

He shoulder'd his mantle of grey otter skin,
And through the wide door, to Sir Erik went in.

'Here sitt'st thou, Sir Erik, in scarlet array'd;
I've wedded thy daughter, the beautiful maid.'

'And who art thou, Rider? What feat hast thou done?
No nidering coward shall e'er be my son.'

'O far have I wander'd, renown'd is my name,
The heroes I conquer'd wherever I came:

'Han Elland, 'tis true, long disputed the ground,
But yet he receiv'd from my hand his death-wound.'

Sir Erik then alter'd his countenance quite,
And out hurried he, in the gloom of the night.

'Fill high, little Kirstin, my best drinking cup,
And be the brown liquor with poison mixt up.'

She gave him the draught, and returning with speed,
'Young gallant,' said he, 'thou must taste my old mead.'

Sir Fridleif unbuckled his helmet and drank;
Sweat sprung from his forehead – his features grew blank.

'I never have drain'd, since the day I was born,
A bitterer draught, from a costlier horn:

'My course is completed, my life is summ'd up,
For treason I smell in the dregs of the cup.'

Sir Erik then said, while he stamp'd on the ground,
'Young knight, 'tis thy fortune to die like a hound.

'My best belov'd friend thou didst boast to have slain,
And I have aveng'd him by giving thee bane:

'Not Helga, but Hela,* shall now be thy bride;
Dark blue are her cheeks, and she looks stony-eyed.'

'Sir Erik, thy words are both witty and wise,
And hell, when it has thee, will have a rich prize!

'Convey unto Helga her gold ring so red;
Be sure to inform her when Fridleif is dead;

'But flame shall give water, and marble shall bleed,
Before thou shalt win by this treacherous deed:

'And I will not die like a hound, in the straw,
But go, like a hero, to Odin and Thor.'

*The goddess of death - according to the Northern mythology.

He cut himself thrice, with his keen-cutting glaive,
And went to Valhalla, the way of the brave.

The knight bade his daughter come into the room:
'Look here, my sweet child, on thy merry bride-groom.'

She look'd on the body, and gave a wild start;
'O father, why hadst thou so cruel a heart?'

She moan'd and lamented, she rav'd and she curst;
She look'd on her love, till her very eyes burst.

At midnight, Sir Erik was standing there mute,
With two pallid corses beside his cold foot:

He stood stiff and still; and when morning-light came,
He stood, like a post, without life in his frame.

The youth and the maid were together interr'd,
Sir Erik could not from his posture be stirr'd:

He stood there, as stiffly, for thirty long days,
And look'd on the earth with a petrified gaze.

'Tis said, on the night of the thirtieth long day,
To dust and to ashes he moulder'd away.

When in 1816 his father had retired to family life in a little house in Willow Lane, Norwich (once the Borrow Museum), George had already assimilated the ways of the outsider. At Tombland Horse Fair he met again with Jasper Petulengro whom he had first encountered near Peterborough some ten years earlier. On that occasion, in the course of a savage reception for trespass upon the Petulengros' camp, Borrow had produced a tame viper secreted in his shirt, an action which earned him the admired sobriquet Sap-engro ('whom snakes obey'). Now as the two made their way to the gypsy tents on Mousehold Heath, Jasper affirmed: 'We are akin'; 'we are *dui palor* – two relations. Your blood beat...as mine always does at the coming of a brother'. Borrow was soon proving himself Lav-engro ('Word Master'), so fluent had he become in Romany.[12]

Willow Lane, Norwich

In polite society Borrow was inclined to conduct himself with an ill grace; he adopted what a friend (Theodore Watts-Dunton) called 'a kind of shy, defiant egoism'[13] to mask the inadequacies he knew were built into his soul. 'I am not fit company for respectable people', he once admitted, having fled (inexplicably) from the presence of fellow dinner guests.[14]

He bore with fits and seizures, and shared with other obsessive personalities a distrust of pleasurable experience. 'It is impossible for a being constructed like myself to be happy for an hour,' he wrote, 'or even enjoy peace and tranquillity'. Borrow confided that images of pleasure and distress 'instantly commence a struggle in my mind, and the gloomy one... invariably prevails.' As a behavioural expert explains it: 'Borrow was able to turn the pleasure of a gift into pain, by doubting the ownership of the gift.'[15] A fragment of verse which Borrow kept by him in the summer-house at Oulton bears ample testimony that – as publishers and readers were to discover – the channels of distrust ran deep:

> To trust a man I never feel inclined,
> Unless I know his very inmost mind;
> Better an open foe your flesh should rend,
> Than you should deem a secret foe your friend.

The two years of hack-work in London, which Borrow embarked upon within a month of his father's death in 1824 and when, coincidentally, his articles with Simpson had expired, brought an early taste of unrewarded ambition. He began a translation into German of a work by his employer, the publisher Sir Richard Phillips, which was abandoned when the text failed to give satisfaction. And he 'was exposed to incredible mortification...from [Phillips'] rage for interference'[16] over the compilation of a six-volume *Celebrated Trials* for which he was paid a niggardly fifty pounds. Another translation (from von Klinger), *Faustus: His Life, Death and Descent into Hell* (1825), was to be burnt by Norwich libraries for containing what the *Literary Gazette* condemned as 'lewd scenes and coarse descriptions'.[17] Near penniless by May 1825, Borrow set off for Salisbury Plain and there began the period of intermittent wanderings whose details he chose to veil. He emerges, in December 1832, an agent for the British and Foreign Bible Society in St Petersburg.

The letter from the Reverend Francis Cunningham, Vicar of Lowestoft, recommending Borrow to the Society introduced him as a person able to read the Bible in thirteen languages while being 'of no very exactly defined denomination of Christians'.[18] Whether he was producing a Manchu edition of the New Testament in Russia, or later in Madrid and Seville reading St Luke's Gospel to groups of female gypsies, proselyte orthodoxy was absent. Indeed, reports to his superiors in London occasioned responses of suppressed consternation, albeit couched in the most decorous drollery: 'You are doubtless a man of very peculiar temperament,' wrote his Society correspondent, Andrew Brandram, 'and we must not apply common rules in judging either of yourself or your affairs'. Having confessed of himself that he was 'of extreme superstitiousness', Borrow had written with a frankness which, said Brandram, 'was what you need not have told [for] it sounded very odd when read aloud in a large Committee'. Commenting on Borrow's meeting with the so-called 'prophetess' of Marzanares, Brandram declared: 'We are odd people, it may be, in England; we are not fond of prophets or prophetesses...Perhaps my wounded pride had not been made whole after the infliction you before gave it by contrasting the teacher of the prophetess with English Rectors'.[19]

72

In the summer of 1839 Borrow persuaded his future wife, Mary Clarke (a devout evangelical and long-time widow), to join him in Seville with her twenty-year-old daughter, Henrietta, so that they would be 'far out of the reach of the malignity of [their] ill-wishers'. After the death of her brother Breame (in May 1837), Mary, who was the owner of Oulton Cottage (through her father's bequest), had found it necessary to re-purchase the mortgage on Oulton Hall, her childhood home, with the purpose of blocking its sale by trustees on behalf of her brother's widow. Marriage to Borrow, whom Mary knew through mutual friends, would be – he told her, perhaps not unknowingly – 'by far the best way of getting possession of an estate'.[20] In Spain she would be under Borrow's protection where, she believed, he was bearing the Gospel armour as a true hero in the cause of Protestantism.

Borrow's predilection for the wild places which drew him was a matter of mounting frustration to his employers. He would absent himself from the cities where duty called, eager for the raw experiences that would inform *I Zincali* (1841), his study of gypsy lore, and the kaleidoscopic *The Bible in Spain* (1843), which was to bring him instant fame. At ease in the company of rogues and rascals, Borrow was quite fearless in the haunts of criminals. He records, for example, how he enjoyed a communal meal taken at a 'hostelry of thieves' on a day when he had thought to deposit a New Testament by the still warm ashes of a bandit fire. Ever alert to Brandram's sensibilities, he reported as being 'without the slightest incident' a journey during which he passed where mounted robbers had earlier bound and shot a mail-coach escort. To his wider audience, the readers of *The Bible in Spain*, Borrow admitted to having watched a dog which 'was gnawing a piece of [this] unfortunate wretch's skull'.

Borrow was possessed of prodigious physical prowess. Elizabeth Barrett recalls his 'six feet three of height, bone and muscle'; she thought him 'fit to be the lion he was'.[21] He is known to have walked the 112 miles from Norwich to London in 27 hours for his interview with the Bible Society, sustained only by the little nourishment that five pence halfpenny could buy; and at the age of fifty he entered thirty-foot waves at Yarmouth to save a sailor when a ship's boat upset.

Sir Walter Scott's biographer, John Gibson Lockhart, thought Borrow's eyes 'full of the fire of genius and enterprise'.[22] Elizabeth Barrett chooses to mention his eyes also: they are 'grey, large, earnest eyes;...he is full of Genius'.[23] (His hair, even as a young man, was 'white as Mont Blanc'.)[24] Watts-Dunton declared that 'there has never before appeared on the English highroads so majestic looking a tramp'.[25]

Lines to Six-Foot Three

A lad, who twenty tongues can talk,
And sixty miles a day can walk;
Drink at a draught a pint of rum,
And then be neither sick nor dumb;
Can tune a song, and make a verse,
And deeds of Northern kings rehearse:
Who never will forsake his friend,
While he his bony fist can bend;
And, though averse to brawl and strife,
Will fight a Dutchman with a knife.

O that is just the lad for me,
And such is honest six-foot three.

A braver being ne'er had birth
Since God first kneaded man from earth:
O, I have cause to know him well,
As Ferroe's blacken'd rocks can tell.
Who was it did, at Suderoe,
The deed no other dar'd to do?
Who was it, when the Boff* had burst,
And whelm'd me in its womb accurst –
Who was it dash'd amid the wave,
With frantic zeal, my life to save?
Who was it flung the rope to me?
O, who, but honest six-foot three!

Who was it taught my willing tongue,
The songs that Braga fram'd and sung?
Who was it op'd to me the store
Of dark unearthly Runic lore,
And taught me to beguile my time
With Denmark's aged and witching rhyme:
To rest in thought in Elvir shades,
And hear the song of fairy maids;
Or climb the top of Dovrefeld,
Where magic knights their muster held?
Who was it did all this for me?
O, who, but honest six-foot three!

Wherever fate shall bid me roam,
Far, far from social joy and home;
'Mid burning Afric's desert sands,
Or wild Kamschatka's frozen lands;
Bit by the poison-loaded breeze,
Or blasts which clog with ice the seas;
In lowly cot or lordly hall,
In beggar's rags or robes of pall,
'Mong robber-bands or honest men,
In crowded town or forest den,
I never will unmindful be
Of what I owe to six-foot three.

That form which moves with giant-grace;
That wild, though not unhandsome, face;

*The Boff is a sudden phenomenon which occurs between the islands of Ferroe, where
seven successive breakers can overwhelm any boat that chances to be in their path.

That voice which sometimes in its tone
Is softer than the wood-dove's moan,
At others, louder than the storm
Which beats the side of old Cairn Gorm;
That hand, as white as falling snow,
Which yet can fell the stoutest foe;
And, last of all, that noble heart,
Which ne'er from honour's path would start,
Shall never be forgot by me –
So farewell, honest six-foot three!

Borrow and Mary – he came to call her Carreta – sailed for London on 3rd April 1840, the patience of Borrow's employers having been exhausted. They were married, a week after disembarkation, at St Peter's, Cornhill, and went directly to Oulton Cottage. Immediately Borrow began to write the version of his life which he chose to call a 'dream', an obfuscation his critics could not forgive. The character he could bear the world to know was Lavengro, the inviolable man of adventure, purged of the insecurities that Borrow was determined to conceal. But *Lavengro* (1851) and its sequel, *The Romany Rye* (1857), failed to please earnest mid-century Victorians who were tiring of Byronic romanticism, and who, after the example of major literary figures – Dickens and Carlyle among them – were seeking to make sense of a maelstrom of change.

At Oulton, where little but the movement of eel catchers and wildfowlers interrupted Borrow's roamings, change came with the rush of smoke and hiss. The railway which Samuel Morton Peto built between Lowestoft and Reedham, and opened in 1847, divided the estate, so that access from Oulton Cottage to the Hall (at long last in Carreta's possession and rented to a farmer) was possible only by means of a footbridge.[26] Borrow, no doubt, felt cornered in a home that never for long contained him.

There were further wanderings in Europe (in 1844); and over an eight-year period (from 1853 to 1860) Borrow covered all of 600 miles in Scotland and 400 in Wales, visiting the remoter outposts of Celtic culture. In the principality, where Carreta and Henrietta joined him, geniality was reawakened. He strode out in cape and with green umbrella, filling the notebook upon which he based *Wild Wales* (1862), a book of 'mellow delights' that has all the 'keenness of observation and feeling for human destiny'[27] that distinguishes *The Bible in Spain*. Few parts of Norfolk were now unknown to him. He paid visits to the philologist Anna Gurney at Northrepps and to Whitwell Elwin, Rector of Booton (near Reepham), the editor of the right-wing *Quarterly Review*. But whenever Borrow was at Oulton, anxieties always returned. He fretted over waning interest in his writings. Increasingly, he was to turn away from a world that, in the slow last decades of his life, came near to forgetting him.

At various times the Borrows deserted Oulton for lodgings at Great Yarmouth: first at 169 King Street; later at 37 Camperdown Place; finally at 24 Trafalgar Place. Whatever the time of year, Borrow swam in the sea. Reporting his rescue of a sailor in September, 1852, *The Bury Post* averred that 'we have known him more than once risk his life for others'. (He liked to record, to Carreta's alarm, how long he could stay under water.) Aged sixty-nine, he swam out, fearless of the dangerous currents, from Lowestoft beach to the Ness buoy far offshore.

Borrow moved his mother in 1849 from Willow Lane to Oulton, where she lived as a tenant into old age. Before her death (from pneumonia) some nine years later, Borrow was impelled by an obsessive desire to prevent it. Day after day he was unable to desist from

75

touching objects – door-knob, chair, floor, bell-rope – 'to which [his] fingers seemed irresistibly drawn'. Touching, he believed, 'baffle[d] the evil chance'.[28] With her death there followed what a biographer has called 'a long diminuendo' in which Borrow lived for a time in the Brompton district of London, where he was taken for a curmudgeon.[29] He published (it seems at his own expense) *Visions of the Sleeping Bard*, mainly a verse translation of a seventeenth-century work, and the word-book of the Romany language, *Romano Lavo-Lil* (1874). Both works went largely unnoticed.

Carreta died in 1869. Henrietta had married. Borrow returned to Oulton to live alone but for the attendance of a housekeeper. (Occasionally he was seen sitting over a tankard of ale in the Norfolk Hotel, in Norwich.) By December 1880 he had ordered a new suit for his burial. He died, a frail man, on 22nd July 1881 and was laid to rest alongside Carreta in Brompton Cemetery.

Oulton had been unaware how notable a man was living nearby. A Mrs Vincent, the daughter of a young working man, records that he kept no servants – a sufficient pointer, she said, for villagers to think 'that he could not be much of a mucher'.[30]

Oulton Cottage, 1840

Algernon Charles Swinburne 1837-1909

Algernon Swinburne remembered being carried as a child from his bed, out through the garden of his grandfather's shooting lodge in Northumberland to the steep place where, beneath a waterfall, was a favourite pool for bathing. What his father so wished him to see that night was no longer a clear pool, but 'one unbroken yellow torrent roaring like continuous thunder'.[1] To Swinburne, who laid his singular gifts at the altar of his feelings, such an elemental thrill was profound.

At Monk's Bay, close to the Swinburnes' home (East Dene) on the Isle of Wight's south-east coast, Algernon first experienced the sensual pleasure of sea-water. He enjoyed what he later described as its life and pulse, its sting and swell, 'which touch and excite the nerves like fire or like music'.[2] He came to look upon the sea as a place of catharsis where, but fleetingly, he found the self-transcendence he craved. 'All his nerves desired the divine touch of it,' admitted the hero of *Lesbia Brandon*,[3] Swinburne's unfinished novel, which contains passages of barely veiled autobiography; soon swimmer and sea have seemingly entered into a mystical union, in which the soul of the sea has possessed him.

So great was his enthusiasm for the sea during the summer of 1868 – 'I am dying for it; there is no lust or appetite comparable'– that, while on holiday at Etretat on the Normandy coast, he overreached himself and was carried out some two miles by treacherous currents. He was brought to land by fishermen in the chance presence of the writer Guy de Maupassant. He also recalls being in difficulties off the Isle of Wight, 'beaten to and fro between the breakers in a furious reflux which flung me back off shore as with the clutch of a wild beast...'[5] Violent seas, it seems, were no deterrent.

It was for the sea-bathing that Swinburne went to Sidestrand, near Cromer, in September 1883 and 1884 in the company of his tenacious friend and rescuer from alcoholic ruin, Theodore Watts-Dunton, who knew the Norfolk coast from childhood holidays and thought the 'stinging saltiness' of its sea-water made it the most buoyant to swim in.[6] His fervour for swimming, it seems, matched Swinburne's. In the novel *Alwyn*, which brought him recognition, Watts-Dunton wrote of 'solitary communings' and of the 'sympathy between the sea and the soul of man.'[7] When Swinburne wrote from Sidestrand to his sister Alice, he warmly commended the bathing as better than at Southwold and told of his delight at being there. 'The whole place,' he said, 'is fragrant with old-fashioned flowers, sweet-william and thyme and lavender and mignonette and splendid with great sun-flowers.'[8]

Evidently Watts-Dunton was happy to cast aside the strict routines he imposed upon Swinburne at his London house, The Pines, on Putney Hill. They lodged with a Mr Jermy, a miller, and his daughter Louie. 'When one [lodger] came in the other went out. It was only by the merest chance that they ever sat down to dinner together. They never gave my [blackberry] puddings a chance,' she recalled.[9]

During his visit Swinburne wrote to his publisher Andrew Chatto expressing surprise that the first instalment of proofs of *A Midsummer Holiday and Other Poems* (1884) had not arrived, and gave direction as to the layout of the pages. The poem he called 'In the Water' was a product of his visit a year earlier:

In the Water

The sea is awake, and the sound of the song of the
    joy of her waking is rolled
From afar to the star that recedes, from anear to the
    wastes of the wild wide shore.
Her call is a trumpet compelling us homeward: if
    dawn in her east be acold,
From the sea shall we crave not her grace to rekindle
    the life that it kindled before,
Her breath to requicken, her bosom to rock us, her
    kisses to bless as of yore?
For the wind, with his wings half open, at pause in
    the sky, neither fettered nor free,
Leans waveward and flutters the ripple to laughter:
    and fain would the twain of us be
Where lightly the wave yearns forward from under
    the curve of the deep dawn's dome,
And, full of the morning and fired with the pride of
    the glory thereof and the glee,

Strike out from the shore as the heart in us bids and
    beseeches, athirst for the foam.

Life holds not an hour that is better to live in: the
    past is a tale that is told,
The future a sun-flecked shadow, alive and asleep,
    with a blessing in store.
As we give us again to the waters, the rapture of
    limbs that the waters enfold
Is less than the rapture of spirit whereby, though the
    burden it quits were sore,
Our souls and the bodies they wield at their will are
    absorbed in the life they adore –
In the life that endures no burden, and bows not the
    forehead, and bends not the knee –
In the life everlasting of earth and of heaven, in the
    laws that atone and agree,
In the measureless music of things, in the fervour of
    forces that rest or that roam,
That cross and return and reissue, as I after you and
    as you after me
Strike out from the shore as the heart in us bids and
    beseeches, athirst for the foam.

For, albeit he were less than the least of them, haply
    the heart of a man may be bold
To rejoice in the word of the sea as a mother's that
    saith to the son she bore,
Child, was not the life in thee mine, and my spirit
    the breath in thy lips from of old?
Have I let not thy weakness exault in my strength,
    and thy foolishness learn of my lore?
Have I helped not or healed not thine anguish, or
    made not the might of thy gladness more?
And surely his heart should answer, The light of the
    love of my life is in thee.
She is fairer than earth, and the sun is not fairer,
    the wind is not blither than she:
From my youth hath she shown me the joy of her
    bays that I crossed, of her cliffs that I clomb,
Till now that the twain of us here, in desire of the
    dawn and in trust of the sea,
Strike out from the shore as the heart in us bids and
    beseeches, athirst for the foam.

Friend, earth is a harbour of refuge for winter, a
    covert whereunder to flee
When day is the vassal of night, and the strength of
    the hosts of her mightier than he;

But here is the presence adored of me, here my desire
    is at rest and at home.
There are cliffs to be climbed upon land, there are
    ways to be trodden and ridden: but we
Strike out from the shore as the heart of us bids and
    beseeches, athirst for the foam.

The undergraduates who welcomed Swinburne's *Poems and Ballads* (1866) and liked to bring a blush to the cheek of passers-by as they chanted his more indecorous verses through the streets, were of a generation for whom the reins of Victorian conformity were fast loosening. Wishing to be thought in tune with post-Darwinian secular progress, they found the religious certainties of childhood (like those enshrined in High Church Tractarianism) easily swept away. There was a mood abroad to shatter, even to ridicule, social and moral convention. As Edmund Gosse, his first biographer puts it, those so minded had discovered in Swinburne 'not merely a poet, but a flag'.[10]

To Swinburne's admirers the chaste and bourgeois verse of Tennyson and his kind had little appeal. They applauded him because his poetry offered an English counterpart to the outpourings of such French exponents of decadence as Théophile Gautier and Charles Baudelaire. Moreover, his verse sounded a heady music. 'Instead of the old, dull iambic measures, the tedium (let us be honest about it) of Wordsworthian blank verse,' writes a modern critic, 'their ears were ringingly assailed by dactyls, anapests, cretics, in a multitude of complex measures; by all sorts of stress variants, which, though they had been used sparingly by earlier poets from Dryden onwards, now appeared moulded with astonishing deftness as the basic metres'.[11]

Swinburne's political sympathies were radical too. As an undergraduate at Balliol (between 1856 and 1860), he was a founder member of an Oxford discussion group, the Old Mortality Society, whose leading light was the republican Scot, John Nichol. Swinburne soon had hanging side by side in his rooms portraits of two champions of Italian freedom, the revolutionaries Giuseppe Mazzini and Felice Orsini. His need for such heroes was acute and would stoke his enthusiasm to a pitch of near-frenzy. He was known to dance before the portrait of Orsini, making 'gestures of adoring supplication';[12] or he would again dance round the table, screaming abuse, while he advocated the Emperor's assassination.[13] Before he met the sixty-one year old Mazzini in London in 1867, the exiled revolutionary had urged him in a letter not to 'lull us to sleep with songs of egotistical love...' but instead to 'shake us, reproach, encourage, insult, brand the cowards, hail the martyrs'.[14] At their meeting Swinburne went down on both knees and kissed Mazzini's hand.

A decision of the Oxford Union – to have a series of murals painted by members of the Pre-Raphaelite Brotherhood in the ceiling bays of its debating chamber – was one of lasting consequence for Swinburne. Of the artists who depicted scenes from Malory's *Morte d'Arthur*, several were to become lifelong friends: Edward Burne-Jones (The Death of Merlin), William Morris (Sir Tristram and Lady Iseult) and Dante Gabriel Rossetti (Sir Lancelot's Vision of the Holy Grail). (It was Rossetti's mural which, in Max Beerbohm's portrayal of Benjamin Jowett, was the subject of the Tutor of Balliol's mischievous inquiry: 'And what were they going to *do* with the Grail when they found it, Mr Rossetti?')[15] Swinburne was captivated by the Pre-Raphaelites' marriage of romanticism and medievalism, and by their fidelity to detail and vivid colour, no less than by the inviolate beauty of their female subjects.[16] Within days of first meeting Morris (who as a boy would ride about the family property in a tiny suit of full armour), Swinburne was composing the six cantos of 'Queen Iseult', the first of his mediaevalist poems.

Among those who viewed the murals were Sir George Otto Trevelyan and his wife Pauline, at whose country seat in Northumberland, Wallington Hall, Swinburne was introduced to their wide circle of literary and artistic friends when he visited from his grandfather's home at Capheaton. Throughout the poet's later torment of ill-advised friend-ships, alcoholism and criticism of his morals, Lady Trevelyan maintained a magnanimous tolerance; she was, her husband acknowledged, 'Algernon Swinburne's good angel.'[17]

The notion embraced by Swinburne, and mirrored in Rossetti's artistic philosophy, of 'art for art's sake' (Gautier's phrase taken up by Baudelaire) sees the goal of art as being the elevation of the human spirit towards an ideal of perfection; and because man is marked by evil, this side of his nature must receive the artist's attention too.[18] It is through self-transcendence, Swinburne believed, and not through reliance upon inspiration – least of all divine inspiration – that the artist creates works of sublime beauty. Having buried the faith of his youth while at Oxford, he was left, he told the American critic E.C. Stedman, with 'nothing but a turbid nihilism.'[19] Then he encountered the writings of Auguste Comte, the Positivist philosopher, and found a God in which he *could* believe.[20] Those 'who worship no material incarnation of any qualities,' he told Stedman, 'may worship the divine humanity, the ideal of human perfection and aspiration, without worshipping any God, any person, any fetish at all'.[21] In Comte's reformist vision man becomes, through the exercise of his intellect, the architect of a Utopian society, in which the restraints imposed by kings and priests upon human freedom are ended.[22] Here, for the atheist Swinburne, was ample encouragement to heap scorn upon Christianity and what he believed to be its absurd superstitions.

Absence of precedent meant that Victorian readers were unprepared for the unbridled blasphemy they encountered in the anti-puritan *Poems and Ballads* (1866) and in *Songs Before Sunrise* (1871). God, who in an earlier verse tragedy *Atalanta in Calydon* (1865) is a malignant oppressor, becomes, in 'A Litany', 'A Christmas Carol' and the 'Hymn to Pro-serpine' *(Poems and Ballads)*, the subject of mockery. In 'Felise' *(Songs Before Sunrise)*, the poet avers that all prayer is pointless since there is no one to hear it; elsewhere, in 'Before the Crucifix' (from the same collection), we find him condemning the 'Christian creeds that spit on Christ' because they have long veiled his true nature.[23] Swinburne concludes with a denunciation of passionate finality: 'Come down, be done with, cease, give o'er;/Hide thyself, strive not, be no more'.[24]

From Hymn to Proserpine
(After the Proclamation in Rome of the Christian Faith)

...For the Gods we know not of, who give us our daily breath,
We know they are cruel as love or life, and lovely as death.
O Gods dethroned and deceased, cast forth, wiped out in a day!
From your wrath is the world released, redeem'd from your chains, men say.
New Gods are crown'd in the city; their flowers have broken your rods;
They are merciful, clothed with pity, the young compassionate Gods.
But for me their new device is barren, the days are bare;
Things long past over suffice, and men forgotten that were.
Time and the Gods are at strife; ye dwell in the midst thereof,
Draining a little life from the barren breasts of love.

I say to you, cease, take rest; yea, I say to you all, be at peace,
Till the bitter milk of her breast and the barren bosom shall cease.
Wilt thou yet take all, Galilean? but these thou shalt not take,
The laurel, the palms and the paean, the breasts of the nymphs in the brake;
Breasts more soft than a dove's, that tremble with tenderer breath;
And all the wings of the Loves, and all the joy before death;
All the feet of the hours that sound as a single lyre,
Dropp'd and deep in the flowers, with strings that flicker like fire.
More than these wilt thou give, things fairer than all these things?
Nay, for a while we live, and life hath mutable wings.
A little while and we die; shall life not thrive as it may?
For no man under the sky lives twice, outliving his day.
And grief is a grievous thing, and a man hath enough of his tears:
Why should he labour, and bring fresh grief to blacken his years?
Thou hast conquer'd, O pale Galilean; the world has grown grey from thy breath;
We have drunken of things Lethean, and fed on the fullness of death.
Laurel is green for a season, and love is sweet for a day;
But love grows bitter with treason, and laurel outlives not May.
Sleep, shall we sleep after all? for the world is not sweet in the end;
For the old faiths loosen and fall, the new years ruin and rend.
Fate is a sea without shore, and the soul is a rock that abides;
But her ears are vex'd with the roar and her face with the foam of the tides.
O lips that the live blood faints in, the leavings of racks and rods!
O ghastly glories of saints, dead limbs of gibbeted Gods!
Though all men abase them before you in spirit, and all knees bend,
I kneel not, neither adore you, but standing, look to the end...

While his father, Captain Charles Henry (promoted admiral in 1867), was absent on naval duties, the boy Swinburne had been largely in the company of a matriarchy comprising his mother Lady Jane (a daughter of the third Earl of Ashburnham), his four sisters, and a cousin who lived nearby. He is said to have inherited his mother's soft voice and 'a rather sing-song intonation', as well as her excitability.[25] Gosse records how 'he had the trick, whenever he grew the least excited, of stiffly drawing down his arms from his shoulders and giving quick vibrating jerks with his hands...At the moment of excitement, he would jerk his legs and twist his feet also'.[26] Furthermore, interlocutors were often irritated by a restless tapping of foot or fingers.

When Swinburne joined Eton in April 1849, fellow Etonians, who could be mercilessly alert to gradations of oddity and the reproach they invite, were soon noticing a tiny boy of delicate physique and sloping shoulders, whose 'great head...was exaggerated by the tousled mass of red hair standing almost at right angles to it'.[27] He walked, they observed, with a peculiar springing step, and spoke in language precociously varied. Contemporary opinion, it appears, was not of one mind about whether the attention Swinburne's singular presence attracted at Eton was inimical. A childhood friend, William Sewell, was adamant that Swinburne was 'fearfully' bullied: 'You might as well give a cockchafer to a boy in the street, and tell him not to spin it, as to put Algernon Swinburne down in the playground of any school, and think he will escape being tormented and baited.'[28] But a cousin (later Lord Redesdale) thought otherwise: that the other boys regarded him 'as a sort of inspired elfin' who belonged 'to another sphere', and 'never thought to interfere with him'.[29]

For all his diligence in classical learning and the long, voluntary hours he spent in the library reading English and European literature, Swinburne's premature departure at the age of sixteen (in 1853), whether or not there was immediate cause, left Eton with few misgivings. We know that, like the poet Shelley ('Mad Shelley'), a predecessor at Eton, Swinburne acquired the sobriquet 'Mad Swinburne'. In adolescence, his impulsive, nervous disposition became a cause of concern to his parents; their son, they were informed by a specialist, was suffering from 'an excess of electric vitality'.[30] What is likely to have disturbed the Eton authorities more was how Swinburne's craving for sensual stimulus found satisfaction – in part, erotic – in the ritual of school birchings, both as voyeur and victim. In one of his numerous flagellant writings, where a beating is being administered at the hand of a dominant female figure, Swinburne has the boy admit to 'tast[ing]...the thrill of pleasure that mingles with the voluptuous agony of the rod'.[31] And among these writings – a number of which have been officially suppressed – are what are taken to be constructs of sham authenticity, but which nonetheless insinuate the unconscionable compliance of Eton masters in Swinburne's pleasures. One such is a letter to the politician and pornographic bibliophile, his friend Richard Monckton Milnes (later Lord Houghton), which tells of a tutor, who, as well as perfuming the room, lets Swinburne stimulate his senses by saturating his face with eau-de-Cologne so that the pain of a beating would be more acute.

Milnes was a deleterious influence upon Swinburne. Much to his own gratification, he encouraged the poet in his exploration of erotic and sado-masochistic literature by making available to him his library at Fryston, in Yorkshire, to which he regularly added the fruits of his covert collecting. (He would, for example, have books from Paris secreted in diplomatic bags properly reserved for despatches to the Foreign Office.)[32] In his reading, notably of the Marquis de Sade, and in particular of his sadistic novel *La Nouvelle Justine, ou les Malheurs de la Vertu* (probably in 1862), with its scenes of sodomy and incest and its pervasive scorn for religion, Swinburne found confirmation of tendencies in his own nature which no longer had the capacity to prompt shame.[33] Milnes, for his part, had no interest in protecting his friend from the hounds of criticism that were gathering about the reputation of a man who, in the cause of art, wished to express the darker truths of human sensuality; instead, he looked for opportunities to introduce Swinburne to those, often in public life, who he knew might be shocked.[34] Gosse records how, after a dinner at Fryston (in 1861) at which James Spedding, then Archbishop of York, and the novelist Thackeray and his daughters were present, Milnes invited Swinburne to read his poem 'Les Noyades'. As the story of a maiden, condemned to be tied naked to a soldier and cast into the sea, moved to its climax in the hearing of the giggling daughters, and with the Archbishop looking on horrified, Milnes's butler saved the girls' further blushes by throwing open the doors to announce: 'Prayers! my Lord!'[35]

As Swinburne's preoccupations gained deeper hold, it took little to trigger an aberrant thought: walking (in August 1872) with his former tutor, Benjamin Jowett, and other Balliol men during a holiday in Grantown-on-Spey, he observed that the Spey was a 'fine rapid river...winding...between banks clothed with broom and wild roses, and with birch enough at hand for the bottoms of all Eton'.[36]

The prudent minority among Swinburne's friends feared that his craving for stimulus would bring about his ruin. Both Jowett, the most steadfast among them, and the Pre-Raphaelite painter William Bell Scott found it hard to detect in him any urgent intellectual inspiration; and the novelist George Meredith, who lived for a short while with Swinburne and Dante Rossetti in London's Cheyne Walk, tellingly disclosed that he did not 'see any internal centre from which springs anything he does'.[37] Faced with the 'storm of moral censure'[38] which raged against him in the literary periodicals, Swinburne succumbed more and more to corrosive pleasures. Lord Lytton, who welcomed him to Knebworth House in August 1866 shortly after *Poems and Ballads* had been temporally withdrawn from sale by its nervous publisher, was soon fearing that Swinburne 'may end prematurely both in repute and in life'.[39]

His drunkenness became a public spectacle. Gosse once observed him tumbling on his hands and knees from a cab in Cheyne Row in the company of the aesthete Walter Pater; and at the Arts Club in Hanover Square (from which he had the grace to resign in August 1870), members were familiar with his drunken 'blasphemy and bawdry' and his noisy harping upon the practices of lesbianism and sodomy.[40] Among Swinburne's drinking companions was the explorer Sir Richard Burton (translator of *The Arabian Nights* and *The Kama Sutra*) and Frederick Hankey, part-author of the sadistic *L'Ecole des biches* and a man who bound obscene books in human skin. To find erotic excitement, which seemed to mean more to Swinburne than the act of copulation itself, he would make visits with Hankey to a flagellant brothel in St John's Wood.

When Swinburne collapsed in the reading-room of the British Museum in July 1868, his father, on doctors' advice, removed him to convalesce at Holmwood, then his home at Shiplake in Berkshire. It was a duty he was to repeat a number of times over the next decade until, in his eighty-first year, and with Swinburne seriously weak from alcoholic dysentery, Watts-Dunton carried him off (in 1878) to Putney to begin the process of reform.

These years before Watts-Dunton's intervention left Swinburne with the emotional scar of a withered friendship. He felt betrayed by Dante Rossetti who was incapable of reciprocating the loyalty of the young men who had idolized him. He was, said the Pre-Raphaelite Val Princep, 'a jealous god' who would not stomach less than an unquestioning discipleship.[41] As Swinburne's moral character deteriorated, there were those, such as the poet Tennyson, voicing their belief that Rossetti, a man of like Bohemian excesses, was materially responsible. In July 1872, Rossetti's son William was advising Swinburne not to visit his father, whose fits of melancholy, insomnia, and drift into schizophrenia, were of grave concern.[42] Rossetti recovered, but his critics, it seems, had had their way: the Swinburne friendship was at an end.

'Oh! the Victorian mustiness of it,' exclaimed a visitor to The Pines,[43] the Putney house which Watts-Dunton (who had met Swinburne through Rossetti) pressed his friend to share with him as sub-tenant. Watts-Dunton and his two sisters provided both attention enough to delight Swinburne's vanity and a life shaped by the orthodox routines of Victorian domesticity. With remarkable ease, Swinburne was persuaded to give up brandy, first for port, then for wine, until, satisfied with beer, he wished for no other.[44] Before long Watts-Dunton had relaxed his guard, seeing that there was no longer need to vet Swinburne's visitors. It was an entirely happy companionship that lasted thirty years, in the course of which Swinburne's revolutionary fires burned low while, increasingly, he wrapped himself in the mantle of a reclusive conservatism.

Prurient interests were not entirely abandoned. In 1892, a correspondence resumed between Swinburne and his recently widowed cousin, Mrs Disney Leith (Mary Gordon) with whom he had played at East Dene as a child. After her engagement in 1864, Swinburne had made known his 'anguished spirit'[45] in 'The Triumph of Time', the poem he was later to describe as 'a monument to the sole real love of his life'.[46] In her earlier letters

84

Mary had reciprocated Swinburne's interest in flagellation and in these re-established exchanges she eagerly did so again. (She was the writer of some ten novels, amongst which *Trusty in Flight* (1893) has the character Freddy subjected to flagellation eighteen times within forty-three pages.)[47] So it was that Swinburne's childhood companion, who in the 1860s had eagerly followed the progress of *Lesbia Brandon*, his novel of bisexual sadism, now found herself the dedicatee of a new birching poem 'Eton: another Ode'.

The literary output of Swinburne's Putney years was considerable. He wrote historical dramas such as *Bothwell* (1874) – a work five times longer than Shakespeare's *Hamlet* – and *Mary Stuart* (1881) which he dedicated to Victor Hugo. His tragedy, *The Duke of Gandia* (1908), is a display of base immorality. Among the poetical works were two further series of *Poems and Ballads* (in 1878 and 1889) and the narratives, *Tristram of Lyonesse* (1882) and *Rosamund, Queen of the Lombards* (1899).

In 1904 Swinburne and Watts-Dunton once again visited the Norfolk coast, this time accompanied by Watts-Dunton's young wife, Clara Reich (at twenty-one, her husband's junior by fifty-two years). On the first day of their stay at Cromer – the 'Haven' of Swinburne's poem – he realised that the sea was now a trial to him. He returned cold and tired to the boat they had hired for swimming in deep water and was content with walking for the rest of the holiday, sometimes alone. One day in his absence, Watts-Dunton paused on his way to the ruined churchyard called locally 'The Garden of Sleep', and sat on the cliff-top in the shade of an empty hut. Some weeks later, news reached The Pines that this same portion of cliff upon which the hut stood had fallen to the sea.[48]

Algernon Swinburne died of pneumonia on 10th April 1909 and was laid to rest at Bonchurch near his childhood home on the Isle of Wight. Against his wishes, he was given a Christian burial.

A Haven

East and north a waste of waters, south and west
Lonelier lands than dreams in sleep would feign to be,
When the soul goes forth on travel, and is prest
Round and compassed in with clouds that flash and flee.
Dells without a streamlet, downs without a tree,
Cirques of hollow cliff that crumble, give their guest
Little hope, till hard at hand he pause, to see
Where the small town smiles, a warm still sea-side nest.

Many a lone long mile, by many a headland's crest,
Down by many a garden dear to bird and bee,
Up by many a sea-down's bare and breezy breast,
Winds the sandy strait of road where flowers run free.
Here along the deep steep lanes by field and lea
Knights have carolled, pilgrims chanted, on their quest,
Haply, ere a roof rose toward the bleak strand's lee,
Where the small town smiles, a warm still sea-side nest.

Are the wild lands cursed perchance of time, or blest,
Sad with fear or glad with comfort of the sea?
Are the ruinous towers of churches fallen on rest

Watched of wanderers woeful now, glad once as we,
When the night has all men's eyes and hearts in fee,
When the soul bows down dethroned and dispossest?
Yet must peace keep guard, by day's and night's decree,
Where the small town smiles, a warm still sea-side nest.

Friend, the lonely land is bright for you and me
All its wild ways through: but this methinks is best,
Here to watch how kindly time and change agree
Where the small town smiles, a warm still sea-side nest.

R. H. Mottram 1883-1971

Ralph Hale Mottram maintained that the leaven informing his writings was an enduring thankfulness for all that middle-class privilege gave him. He would look down from a window seat of the family's home – above Gurney's Bank in Norwich – and feel the pathos of the wage-earners who paraded on Bank Plain below in their respites from late-Victorian drudgery.[1] With little but 'beer and prayer' to keep them from 'violent revolution',[2] he opined, theirs was a 'poor little leisure' to compare with his own, filled as their lives were 'with such second-rate, derivative opportunity and enjoyment'.[3] To Mottram, contemplating the youthful impressions he recollects in *The Window Seat* (1954), they 'might have been denizens of another world'.[4]

In Norwich's social hierarchy, the Mottrams stood 'just below the level of the learned professions'.[5] Ralph's father, James, like the two generations before him, was chief clerk to the bank's partners, a position which provided the means to support in comfort, yet with no hint of ostentation, a domestic household consisting of a cook, four maids, a washerwoman and a boy.[6] His mother, Fanny Ann, much liked by the servants for her progressive ways – 'It's no good, James, the servants must have higher wages and regular evenings off, otherwise they won't stay...'[7] – fulfilled the humane obligations she believed were placed upon a woman of her standing. Hers was an innate benevolence expressed in good works, particularly amongst the poor who lived in the city's yard dwellings. Rather than 'go calling on middle-class mediocrity', Mottram tellingly recalls, '...she went out to do battle... [carrying] a sheaf of soup tickets in one hand and a bundle of cast-off clothes in the other'.[8]

Both Mottram's parents were imbued with a creedless, free-thinking tolerance long nourished by family attendance at the Octagon Unitarian Chapel in Colegate, from whose pulpit Mottram remembers hearing little of individual salvation, but much of the doctrine of 'social betterment' under an 'immanent' God.[9] In 'reaching out' to the disadvantaged, Fanny was doing what her understanding of religious duty made paramount.

Looking back to the turn of the century in *Vanities and Verities* (1958), Mottram remembers the people at the foot of society's ladder, with no rungs within reach. There were the 'loafers', incapable of employment, 'whose skin was visible through their horrible swathings and footgear', and crossing-sweepers who looked no better.[10] The labouring poor had their own uniform of disrepute – the 'stained, stinking coverings'[11] from which noses were quickly averted. No one, not even the women of refinement, could be immune to indecorous realities. Their voluminous skirts habitually trailed through the horse-droppings, the mud or powdery dust.[12]

At the appearance of 'titled and landed folk'[13] near-mediaeval deference held sway. Mottram instances the arrival of carriages during the Triennial Music Festival, and how they drew 'a dingy multitude' to St Andrew's Plain and the neighbouring streets, eager for the spectacle of departure. To cries of 'the Earl of Albemarle's carriage' or 'Lady Canterbury's carriage stops the way!'[14] the 'notables' dispersed from St Andrew's Hall, bright stars against a grinding drabness.

Mottram, who was elected Lord Mayor of Norwich in coronation year (1953), regretted the loss of Society's influence upon the affairs of the city in the early years of the new century. Society, he admitted, had its 'flimsy, pretentious surface',[15] its self-regarding snobberies, but for all its faults, he knew that it had served Norwich's many bodies – civic, educational and altruistic – with an effectiveness that later bureaucracies rarely matched.

R. H. Mottram

Afternoon Tea

AH! How do you do?   (The game begins!
Do my eyes show how my heart must bleed?
Yours don't, or you doctor them wonderfully...dear!)
Who is he?...with the head like a pear,
And the indrawn cheeks of a...Gondolier?
He founded a Home for the Fishless Finns!
Who, he thought, were about to disappear;
Yes...quite original...guaranteed!

(How many times, how many weeks,
Must we meet like this?...I know there's fun
In all illicit things...but it palls.
When I think I have only just begun
To make you feel...the curtain falls
From your eyes...in the midst of this crowd, we're one,
And our secret's safe...except for your cheeks,
Where the spirit of all temptation speaks
As plain as if, at some recognised shrine,
We'd been sanctioned by all these...swine!)

Must I take this cup to the Dowager?
Too bad...He! he! (across the room
Our eyes converse...do you look at her
Jealous...? I said 'The Dowager,'
And so she is, for me.) The bloom
On those hydrangeas, isn't it fine?
Two lumps, if you please. Dear me, it's wet!
...I saw him on Thursday, he seemed quite well!
(To prove I mean love, I'd burn in Hell!)

Come out to the garden...September's here!
The Links are close...they've a capital view!
(A dove-coloured rain-cloud's abrush with the blue,
But all the humid lawn and wood,
Scented and flashing, now they're soaked,
And redolent always of Love and you,
Won't heal the hurt of your eyes!...) I choked
With laughing nearly...Wasn't it good!

(Eyes, I know what you mourn to say,
We have argued it all before!
You think it will spoil what I have to do?
Some manhood I've pretensions to,
Better than anyone you know,
What's a man called who shirks a risk?
I may win or lose...meanwhile I throw...
Better to sink in the void with you,

Than survive alone to find the shore!)
The head is fine, but, in its way,
I prefer the one with the disc!

(That blouse of yours, the colour of cream,
With lace that froths right up to your ear...)
He walks as if he went by steam!
Ha! ha! (Could you disrobe, my dear
From that, as easily as your eyes
Let slip your naked soul, what a dream
Of neck and shoulder you'd lay bare!)
A pretty room, that dado, now,
Is really...(Darling, if you dare
To screw up your lips like that I'll kick
Prudence, the sneak, to his master, Nick!)
...Thank you, it's most refreshing!...(How
Do I find my tea? You touch the cup
With one slim finger...I'll drink it up
Though it be blood!)...The eye can roam
So restfully on that weather-worn,
Moss-covered old red barn, with its vane...
Might be a Morland?...say Old Crome!
(Suddenly dumb!...why, I'd be slain
To bring the mischief back to your face,
If only that bubble of dainty lace
You call your handkerchief were torn
To tie up the bleeding place!...
But you're a woman...O the scorn!)

A piece of cake!...(Again you plead;
You only inspire an hour's lust,
Then fall forever...a thing of use,
Mortgaged away. If what you need
Is this performance twice a week
Till you are seventy...Well! you must!
Pour out tea to your heart's disgust...
Amid chatter of fools...can you deduce
This as your destiny?)

(Look at the pale ethereal cloud
That topples heavily, and shows
The murky side of Heavenly snows,
A cloud's disgrace...but it helps the grass
To live! And we? We boast...and pass
For never having quite allowed
Nature to have her will with us!...
She *is* so...miscellaneous.
- In fact, by our advice, impure...
Pray, what is Purity?...Who knows?)

No, thank you, I'd much rather walk.
(O pretty blush!) The barn? (Again!
You're all confusion...for you can see
I refused a lift, in order to be
Allowed to stay with you...and talk,
And you wish to stay and...talk, with me.)

Thank you, no, it's out of my way!
(I'll tell you what we'll do, one day,
We'll give Society the slip,
And dress you up in a pinafore,
Then you shall teach me how to skip, ...
I'll skip till you can't laugh any more, ...
And smother you in the hay!)

Good-bye, Mr...much better, thanks!
Quite convalescent!...(There they go,
As dribbles off the mountain flanks
The weary weight of winter snow...
And Spring, our Spring, is here...and so...

When Mary comes in to take the tray,
I'd like to tell her, dear old soul,
The reason why, day after day,
She finds me loitering, when the whole
Of the company's gone, is that I stay
To be drowned in your fits of glum despair,
Cling to the hope of a kiss I stole,
So waked to life by the raillery
In your eyes and voice...at last to be
Caught and burned alive in your hair!)

The first of Mottram's schools, which his younger brother Hugh also attended, was the girls' establishment, one of 'gentility and advanced culture',[16] run by their mother's friends, Maria and Katie Clark, enlightened pioneers in the provision of liberal opportunity for young ladies in Norwich. Behind high walls near Surrey Street – where had stood the palace named by the third Duke of Norfolk after his son Henry Howard, the poet Earl of Surrey – the school occupied a Georgian building of labyrinthine rooms and passages through which Mottram never tired of roaming. As well as cherishing all its 'gay, forward-looking vitality',[17] his time there, he said, sowed in his mind an idea of 'remarkable influence', namely that 'every ill to which mankind, or more especially woman-kind, was liable, was remediable'.[18]

Then, at Dr Wheeler's Paragon House School, on Earlham Road – later to be Bracondale School – where the children were those of mostly Nonconformist middle-class aspirants, Mottram encountered an altogether more robust challenge. Amongst 'individualists of an undiluted type',[19] as he called them, he began to shed the complacencies of privilege. Hindsight taught him that it was a process not completed until the First World War.

From the outset of his own service with Gurney's Bank, still spoken of as such but owned now by Barclays, Mottram knew that banking would never be his *forte*. He made, he said, 'a sorry...fist of what was my plain hereditary duty'.[20] The treadmill of repetitive tasks and the slow, impatient waiting upon promotion – for it took eight years to be entrusted with a ledger – shaped the period between 1900 and 1927, years interrupted only by war. Within months of immediate enlistment in the Royal Norfolk Regiment, Mottram had found the pluck to 'summon my voice from my boots',[21] as he put it, and make a fair success of drilling men – on the strength of which he was made corporal.

After sketchy training, Mottram embarked in September 1915 for Flanders as a junior officer in Kitchener's New Armies, then engaged in the Loos offensive; his father, in his last illness, was not to see him again. Like others, he was to notch up the inevitable firsts within a matter of hours. There was the whine and explosion of shells as he arrived at the Poperinghe railhead; then, bursts of gunfire keeping him low in a hedge, when to his astonishment, the one-armed General Congreve, wearing two V.C. ribbons, passed by in the open on a fine mare; and then – only too soon – the cry of 'stretcher-bearer' from below the parapet of a firebay.[22] In his *Ten Years Ago* (1928), *Through the Menin Gate* (1932) and elsewhere, Mottram was to capture trench warfare in all its grave reality.

Providence, he felt, played a kindly hand when Brigade Intelligence discovered that he was the one person who could make himself understood in the French common to the people of the Franco-Belgian border. Removed from the front line as an intelligence officer, he was given the task of establishing fair play between the army and the inhabitants of the villages and small towns upon whom the combatants were billeted.[23] And away from the stutter of machine guns, 'Send for the intelligence officer!' no doubt summoned him like an echo of reprieve.

Up to the Line

Stand to! For Dusk descending
Is torn with fusillade,
And we must go from Wypers Town
To bring our fellows aid;

Fall in! No bugle sounded
Heartens the Hanger-back,
As, heavy burdened, closely girt,
We foot the shell-marked track.

Steady in front! To one there comes
The Great Fall-out, and Last!
The stretcher holds his blood-soaked clay,
And we go stumbling past,

And, Mother dear, in England,
Pray for a Soldier Son,
Whose voice must guide two hundred men,
Whose heart beats faint for one!

Mottram remembers the summer evening he spent drafting the title poem of his first collection, *Repose and other Verses* (1906) – published under the *nom de plume* J. Marjoram – as being one of unsuppressed emotion. He would look back upon the experience and its 'milder repetitions' as being moments of spiritual indwelling which, he disclosed, had 'strewn a fragrance all through my otherwise fairly commonplace, if happy life...'[24] Fortuitously, he had the opportunity to show his finished verses to Ada Galsworthy, the future novelist's wife, when she visited his father in his capacity as trustee of her first marriage settlement. From John Galsworthy, who became Mottram's mentor, he received 'the generous and patient guidance'[25] which sustained him through nearly twenty years of unrewarded endeavour until the appearance, in 1924, of his Hawthornden Prize novel, *The Spanish Farm*. Along the way, it seems, Galsworthy had need to avert despair: 'If you [give up writing] you'll experience a kind of starvation,'[26] he advised. Moreover, he made himself responsible for seeing *The Spanish Farm* placed with the publisher Chatto and Windus who agreed to publish on the condition that Galsworthy wrote a preface for which he would receive no fee. Described by him as a 'landscape with figures', the novel tells of one Madeleine Vanderlynden, a Flemish farmer, who lives within range of German guns in the Flanders of the 1914-18 War. Together with *Sixty-Four, Ninety-Four* (1925) – 'Sixty-four, ninety-four, He'll never go sick any more, The poor beggar's dead' – and *The Crime at Vanderlyndens* (1926), it was reissued in 1927 as *The Spanish Farm Trilogy*. Ten thousand copies sold in very quick time, securing for Mottram, at the age of forty-three, the 'literary place that satisfied [him]'.

When he left the Bank's foreign desk for the last time, in November 1927, to live by writing, he was never to have misgivings, least of all financial ones; his published works were to number fifty-five. Amongst them were books on banking, a biography of the painter, *John Crome of Norwich* (1931), and the topographical *East Anglia* (1933) and *The Broads* (1952). And through the 1930s, and well into the post-war period, Mottram carried a heavy burden as lecturer and occasional broadcaster. (During the Second World War, when he was appointed to maintain morale among British and American Forces in East Anglia, he delivered as many as 253 lectures to the military alone in the single year 1942.)

Mottram was a Norwich man *par excellence*. No one more singularly portrayed its life and character, or welcomed the prosperity of its burgeoning professional class fast establishing itself – in all its concentric association – within the city's new-built suburbs. And unsurprisingly, the places in which Mottram and his wife Madge brought up their family were, with one brief and unavoidable exception, these same leafy totems of success. Newly-wed at the time of the Armistice (in 1918), they shared with Mottram's mother the family house which his father had bought in retirement, The Birches on Bracondale, then home to the first of the retired professional people who chose to live beyond the city walls. Their first independent home, in Cecil Road, which Mottram bravely purchased with slender post-war resources out of consideration for his ageing mother, was, of necessity, a mean one. Thereafter, but for the last months of his life, they lived in Poplar Avenue in the house designed by his brother Hugh and situated west of the Newmarket Road where a nursery garden had sloped to the Yare. 'Across the western angle of the sitting room'[27] Hugh incorporated in a square bay the most treasured of his brother's window seats, from which Mottram looked south to Colney Hall and to the high trees of Keswick Wood beyond.

A cottage on the next-door plot, which Fanny Mottram intended to occupy, was never built. She died in 1925, aged seventy-two, when her son's family had barely settled in. In her memory, the Mottrams' gardener transplanted a seedling copper beech which she had nurtured at The Birches. Now no longer there, Mottram records how it grew to be 'as good an epitome as could be found for all the beauty she saw in and drew from life.'[28]

Mottram valued the pleasure of physical work which drew him away from the writing desk. With typical exactness, he calculated as being 175 the average number of early afternoons each year he gave to the Poplar Avenue garden and to the orchard established on Fanny's erstwhile plot.[29] The planting was unashamedly profuse and the cropping heavy. 'We have', he recorded, 'the whole gamut of arboreal state around us'.[30] Against the sitting room wall flourished the offspring of a fig tree which had grown in the Duke of Norfolk's Surrey House garden; to the east stood a 'tree of Heaven'; on the front lawn, a mulberry. Every 30th October, his birthday, Mottram would meticulously list the harvest: 'the sacks of potatoes, the nuts and medlars, the apples and the pears that we lay by'.[31] Special to him were the Belle de Louvain plums hanging in August 'with purple fruit the size of gooses' eggs'.[32] And all the while 'the detritus...of literary activity' was gathering in a summer-house.[33]

As children, Ralph and Hugh were regularly taken to Overstrand on Norfolk's bracing 'Poppyland' coast, then a natural choice of middle-class parents new to the experience of holidaying away from home. From rented cottage rooms, to which they had to fetch water in pails, they walked the Cromer clifftops blowing with wild flowers, to the mill at Side-strand, and among the rhododendrons of Northrepps woods. By the time that Mottram first returned there with his own children in the late 1920s, Lords Battersea and Hillingdon had bought tracts of the once open land.[34] The mill was gone; Sidestrand's deserted church tower had fallen (in 1916) to the sea. Now they paid visits to Lady Battersea – a Rothschild – who had met Fanny during the First World War. Her house, The Pleasaunce, with its maze of rooms and red brick cloisters, possessed among its fine collection of political portraits those of Gladstone and Baldwin. With her death, The Pleasaunce became a rest home in whose 'hardly recognisable sitting room' Mottram once lectured to troops.[35] In his early seventies, he wrote of Overstrand: 'I still feel able to escape the imprisonment of myself in myself there.'[36]

The Deserted Church Tower On Sidestrand Cliff

Oh! once I had a clamorous bell
The villagers all knew so well
That through my porch they drifted in;
To learn the ways of shunning Sin.
For 'Love wide as the Sea' their quest,
For 'Peace' and 'Everlasting Rest!'
They sang and sat with one accord,
The preacher preached, the elders snored,
The children fidgeted and played
And each young man eyed each young maid,
Till when he came to 'Glory be...'
All rose, and drifted out of me!

My bell is gone, my porch is down;
Through my void windows now is blown
By every wind the day may send
The breath no preacher now will spend.

> The young and old are here in rows,
> Where, flowery tall, the sweet hay grows;
> They neither fidget now nor snore,
> The young men eye young maids no more;
> They come not, go not, soon or late,
> But with me, on the cliff-edge, wait.
> Seaward we slip, and seem more fain
> To be 'washed clean' and 'born again'!

Over a long life Mottram served on many professional bodies and travelled widely to attend formal luncheons and dinners. (He fully endorsed a remark of Russell Colman, of Colman's of Norwich, who said, 'London is a wonderful city and the finest building in it is Liverpool Street Station.') At Carpenters' Hall he recalls Hilaire Belloc 'wav[ing] away... the most peerless hock'[37] on account, Mottram supposed, of its being German. And while the Canadian Authors' Association was being entertained at the Mansion House, he saw how Kipling's eyebrows would 'mount and mount'[38] as speeches threatened to overrun.

Honours came Mottram's way too. He was a fellow of the Royal Society of Literature, a member of its Council and sometime Treasurer. At the inaugural congregation of the University of East Anglia in 1966, which installed Lord Franks as Chancellor, both he and the historian, Professor Asa Briggs, received honorary Doctorates of Letters.

Mottram had wanted to live by poetry, yet 'stumbled into prose fiction'[39]because it was 'marketable'. The verses which had impressed Galsworthy were soon followed by *New Poems* (1909). Much later there appeared – under his own name – *Poems New and Old* (1930), largely a re-issue of the two earlier collections, together with poems written before 1917. In its preface, he concedes that poetry as 'an effective means of expressing what one felt, does not seem to have survived my promotion to the rank of Sergeant.' Nevertheless, Mottram felt that 'the kind things' which were said about the early poems had 'sealed [his] career';[40] his place in the sun, earned with the success of *The Spanish Farm* after years of 'utter failure and obscurity',[41]remained secure through a writing life which lasted well into his eighties.

W. H. Auden 1907-1973

Arriving for the first time to board at his Surrey preparatory school – St Edmund's, Hindhead – Wystan Hugh Auden's opening remark all but shook the 'monumental poise' of the matron: 'I like to see the various types of boys,'[1] he declared. The young schoolboy, it seems, had early established the detachment which so characterised his poetry. Auden was, as his friend the poet Stephen Spender explains it, an observer of both his own life and the lives of others as if 'from the wings'[2] and, as one who loved moorland and fell, he would often adopt the perspective of great height: 'Consider this and in our time/as the hawk sees it or the helmeted airman'.[3]

The 'dream country'[4] of Auden's childhood was the machinery of the industrial sites near his home in Solihull, and beyond in the limestone landscape of the Pennine mines. Here were 'beautiful machines that never talked/But let the small boy worship them and learn/All their long names whose hardness made him proud'.[5] He welcomed them into his imaginative world, where he moved among them as 'sole autocrat',[6] entirely content with their unreciprocable companionship.

His father, Dr George Auden, who at Cambridge had taken a First in Natural Sciences and who was Birmingham's first School Medical Officer, willingly procured the books on geology and mining that Wystan craved. And when, at the outbreak of war in August 1914, his father joined the Royal Army Medical Corps and sold the family house, Wystan's interests were still accommodated. Living in rooms rented by his mother Constance in various parts of the country during school holidays, he would venture down mines in the company of his two elder brothers, visit slate quarries in Wales or seek out disused lead mines on the moors.[7]

The subject of Auden's poem 'Allendale', an item of juvenilia, lies in the lead mining district of Alston in Cumberland.

Allendale

The smelting-mill stack is crumbling, no smoke is alive there,
Down in the valley the furnace no lead ore of worth burns;
Now tombs of decaying industries, not to strive there
    Many more earth-turns.

The chimney still stands at the top of the hill like a finger
Skywardly pointing as if it were asking: 'What lies there?'
And thither we stray to dream of those things as we linger,
    Nature denies here.

Dark looming around the fell-folds stretch desolate, crag-scarred,
Seeming to murmur: 'Why beat you the bars of your prison?'
What matter? To us the world-face is glowing and flag-starred,
    Lit by a vision.

W.H. Auden during his school-days

So under it stand we, all swept by the rain and the wind there,
Muttering: 'What look you for, creatures that die in a season?'
We care not, but turn to our dreams and the comfort we find there,
  Asking no reason.

When he turned to mapping the human landscape, Auden found his father the best of guides. Reading the works of Freud and Jung – which he was encouraged to do – the adolescent son was soon keenly reciprocating his father's 'systematic curiosity'[8] about the causes of human behaviour. This psychological interest chimed with a temperament eager to synthesise unruly webs of human motivation; and in the company of his friends he would indulge, sometimes to their discomfort, the sense of control that his 'knowingness' permitted him.[9] As early as 1917, at the time of Auden's precocious entry to the top form of St Edmund's at the age of ten, Christopher Isherwood (his later literary collaborator) had been struck by his fellow pupil's 'tantalizing air of knowing disreputable...secrets'; with his hints of 'forbidden knowledge and stock of mispronounced scientific words...he enjoyed among us...the status of a kind of witch-doctor.'[10]

At Gresham's – the public school in the north Norfolk town of Holt, which he joined in September 1920 – Auden would explore the origins of human motives and passions in conversation with friends. 'Wystan did not talk like a boy,' the poet John Pudney (a near-contemporary) recalls, but in language '...mature, worldly, intellectually challenging.'[11] Michael Davidson, the brother of the school's violin teacher, of whom Auden spoke as 'the first adult homosexual he had met', found the maturity of 'even his smallest remarks ...alarming.'[12]

97

In choosing Gresham's for his son, George Auden no doubt wished to see Wystan's interest in science further encouraged, something which the school, with its modern curriculum – almost shorn of classics – was well qualified to do. Soon, though, it was not the 'excellently equipped' laboratories that were the focus of his interest, but the library, which he thought was 'perhaps the only requisite because real people, who can learn...will teach themselves.'[13] Meanwhile, a friend's chance remark 'One afternoon in March at half-past three' was the agent of revelation:

> Kicking a little stone, he turned to me
> And said, 'Tell me, do you write poetry?'
> I never had, and said so, but I knew
> That very moment what I wished to do.[14]

Reading Walter de la Mare's verse anthology *Come Hither*, Auden was excited to discover how poetry could admit so great a variety of stylistic forms and need not be serious to be good.[15] Before long he was producing a steady stream of verse – influenced in the main by his reading of Thomas Hardy ('For more than a year I read no-one else'), Wordsworth and Robert Frost – and sending examples home with his letters on paper torn from exercise books.

Auden shunned corporate activities where his attendance was not a matter of obligation. And whenever communal life vexed him, he would go off early in the morning on solitary walks, eager for their introspective consolations. One day, on the edge of the salt marsh some miles from Gresham's, he watched a snowstorm blow in from the sea towards Salthouse; at Weybourne the school's naturalist saw him on several occasions on the shingle beach staring out to sea. As Auden later understood, the introvert adolescent, conscious that his unpopularity or inferiority is deserved, will turn 'away from the human to the non-human' to seek solace in the mute observation of the natural world; furthermore, 'art for him', as it was for Auden himself, 'will be something infinitely precious, pessimistic, and hostile to life.'[16]

In retrospect, Auden did not regard his time at Gresham's as an unhappy period. He thought the school mercifully free of the tribal intolerances rife in less civilised schools. That corporal punishment, bullying, swearing and smuttiness were practically unknown was due in large part to the operation of the 'Honour System' (as it was called). But the system had other consequences which made him doubt its wisdom. Devised as the means by which behaviour amongst the boys was self-regulated, it was sustained through appeals to their inherent feelings of loyalty to an institution proud of its moral rectitude. Meanwhile, for its proper working, the boys were expected – in the last resort – to report certain types of offence, and so renege on the schoolboys' once inviolable code of honour. Auden felt that the moral life of the community was thereby based on fear, not least because of 'the temptation...offered to the natural informer'.[17] And in the matter of boys' undeveloped emotions, particularly sexual ones, the Honour System seemed in large part designed to ensure their utter suppression, a cheerless and harmful outcome presented as spurious virtue in many a school chapel sermon.

Under Auden's bachelor headmaster, J. R. Eccles, described by the school's historian as 'dedicated...a little pedantic...[and] seemingly without ambition and without great vision'[18] there were a few masters to whom he felt 'an immense debt'.[19] The music master, Walter Greatorex, whose friendship Auden regarded as his first 'with a grown up person',[20] was appreciated both for his musicianship and for combining 'haughty indifference with the greatest kindness and tact',[21] as Auden's friend and contemporary Robert Medley saw it. From C. H. Tyler, the senior classics master, he believed he had learned 'more about poetry and the humanities than from any course of University lectures'[22] and Frank McEachran was remembered for his engaging choice of literary extracts which he expected the boys to recite with passion while standing on chairs.[23] An effective schoolmaster himself in the 1930s, Auden could be brutally perceptive in his assessment of university men attracted to teaching: 'only too often [they are] those who are afraid of the mature world, either the athletic whose schooldays were the peak of their triumph from which they dread to recede, or else the timid academic whose qualifications or personal charm are insufficient to secure them a fellowship; in either case the would-be children'.[24] Here, in Auden's unflinching analysis, we see exemplified the icy discernment that characterised him.

Not until after Robert Medley had left Gresham's for art school at the end of 1922, did he become aware of the strength of Auden's romantic feelings for him. In the course of a visit he paid Auden at his parents' house, there came to George Auden's notice a poem written by his son which the friends had been discussing and which he suspected of having an erotic content. Their assurances that the relationship was merely platonic was the end of the matter.[25] When Medley considered the schoolboy friendship years later, he put on record an incident in the school swimming pool – where the boys went naked – in which Auden, diving piggyback from the top board as Medley's passenger, suffered a bleeding nose; it was, Medley revealed, 'as near as we...ever got to an embrace at Gresham's'.[26]

The poem which had unsettled Dr Auden he destroyed. Another, from the same period, is thought to refer to a holiday Auden and Medley spent together in Yorkshire:

> Who deafened our ears during those days,
> Who dulled our eyes,
> That life's great doxology we failed
> To recognize?
>
> No whisper fell when we watched the wheel
> Toss at the mill:
> 'You never knew days richer than these,
> Nor ever will.'
>
> Then standing at sundown on the cliff,
> It fired your hair;
> No voice said to me: 'You will not find
> Two souls as rare.'

According to another Greshamian, John Pudney, Auden fell in love with him 'and said so very decorously'.[27] They were companions on walks, sometimes in summer to a farmhouse where Auden would order a tea of eggs and strawberries and cream. Hempstead Mill and the Hangs, a valley to the north of the school, were favourite haunts. One afternoon Pudney witnessed his friend throwing a sheaf of poems into a pond in the school woods – seemingly in a momentary expression of self-deprecation.[28] Deputed the same evening to stand watch, Pudney saw Auden wade into the near-stagnant water to retrieve his manuscript which, all along, he had sought to protect by wrapping it in some kind of waterproof material.

Big School at Gresham's

Auden was in the habit of sending all his poems to Michael Davidson, then in his mid-twenties and working as a journalist in Norwich. Invariably they were returned annotated with suggestions. Though Davidson made sexual advances, their friendship remained chaste, 'not on moral grounds,' Auden said, but because he did not find him physically attractive.[29] (Years later, when Davidson was drawn to the island of Ischia by the availability of local boys, he visited Auden at the property the poet had bought there as a summer retreat for himself and his lover, Chester Kallman; 'I...listened with awe and only a little understanding to [Auden's] intellectually spatial orations',[30] he wrote.)

In 1925, during his last spring term at Gresham's, Auden wrote an elegy (which he sent to Davidson) on a schoolboy who had died as a result of a fall from a tree:

> The wagtails splutter in the stream
> And sparrows quarrel round the door,
> We have not woken from the dream
> Its wonder stirs us as before;
> But one of us will never bring
> His music to a latter spring.
>
> He found the earliest thrushes' nest
> Before us all; his was a grace
> Like poplars with their leaves at rest
> Or pony in the wind; his face
> Was keen with solitude, to fears
> And griefs unknown in sixteen years.
>
> That spring was early and the time
> Was swift with us from day to day
> Far into April, till his climb
> To look into a squirrel's drey.
> The rotten branches bore him well
> For he had reached it when he fell.

100

Three weeks he lay and watched a rook
Or lilac hanging in the rain,
A pair of wrynecks came and took
The nesting box outside the pane
And hatched their brood; the first one cried
Upon the morning that he died.

No dogs barked in the street below
The churchyard where they dug his grave,
The day wore nothing strange to show
That earth took back the dust she gave,
And cuckoos they were calling still
When we had left him in the hill.

The undergraduates of Auden's Oxford generation recognised in him an intellect both rare and daunting. In conversation he would deliver his pronouncements – 'new anathemas, new hosannas' his tutor Nevill Coghill once called them[31] – in language rich in the unfamiliar terminology of science and psychology and gleaned from the more esoteric regions of the *Oxford English Dictionary*. The poet Cecil Day-Lewis (then reading Greats at Wadham) tells of his 'intellectual bossiness' and how he tried to organise the lives of his friends.[32]'He forced issues too much, made everyone too conscious of himself...'[33] observed Stephen Spender, who (in 1928) printed Auden's first volume of poems on his own hand-operated press. Spender doubted if Auden ever succeeded in breaking away from the 'isolation in human relationships' into which his 'overwhelming cleverness' cast him.[34]

Whenever Louis MacNeice called on Auden in his rooms in Peckover Quadrangle at Christ Church, he sensed that Auden had been busy 'getting on with the job',[35]an early indication of the punctiliousness that in later life would often appear obsessive. And so long as he was able to maintain the discipline necessary for the prosecution of his work, disorder elsewhere in his habits of life mattered little to him. A crumpled untidiness became, with the passing years, something he appeared to flaunt: 'the most dishevelled child of all disciplinarians'[36]was Kallman's judgment of him. Auden's hosts attuned themselves to a guest with a manifest disregard for house-training: he would scatter tobacco ash wherever he went and, having left burn marks on furniture, would offer only a perfunctory apology; he invariably shovelled his food and during the night would raid the refrigerator for left-overs. An eccentricity seemed to matter less: bemused hosts would discover his bed piled with curtains and carpets – even on one occasion, all topped with a large framed picture.[37]

When Auden left Oxford in 1928, it was with a Third Class degree. A fellow pupil of Nevill Coghill observed that 'literature as a subject for analytical dissection'[38]had not interested him; Stephen Spender thought Auden had overworked in the period immediately before his Finals. For a year he was in Berlin, freely abandoning homosexual restraint with a series of boys he met in the bars there. When Christopher Isherwood (a lover since 1925) paid him a number of visits, there began a literary collaboration that was to see the publication of a series of plays: *The Dog Beneath the Skin* (1935), *The Ascent of F6* (1936) and *On the Frontier* (1938). 'For years we fucked like rabbits evey chance we got,'[39]Isherwood declared of a relationship which continued at intervals until 1939.

In the summer of 1930 Auden took up schoolmastering, an occupation in which he could maintain the routines of a writer's life. Larchfield Academy (where he taught for one year) was a small private school, somewhat run-down, situated in Helensburgh on the Clyde. 'We...could not quite get the measure of him,'[40]recalled one of his pupils, though with rebels and underdogs there was sympathetic rapport. Then at the Downs School – situated beneath the ridge of the Malvern Hills at Colwall – which he thought an energetic, Boy Scout kind of place, there occurred an experience of spiritual profundity. In the company of colleagues out on the lawn after dinner, he felt the power of transcendental indwelling which, for the time of its duration, dispelled for him the shame of 'my greeds and self-regard.' 'For the first time in my life I knew exactly – because, thanks to the power, I was doing it – what it means to love one's neighbour as oneself'. The memory, he said, made all later self-deception 'much more difficult.'[41]

During Auden's year at Larchfield, his *Poems* (1930), which included several from Spender's 1928 private printing, was accepted for publication by T.S. Eliot, the editor at Faber and Faber. Though the poems are striking in their range of images and styles,[42]they were not warmly greeted by reviewers who thought Auden disposed towards obscurity, a view iterated by many who followed the progress of his prolific muse. In defence of *Poems*, the *Adelphi* believed that Auden 'expresses thought stripped to essentials' – thought that, in its exactness, conveys its 'strict emotion'.[43]

In a work he completed at Colwall, *The Orators: An English Study* (1932) – a fragmentary notebook in prose and poetry – Auden unpicks the angst of male solidarity that, as the 1930s developed, was to evoke 'the fantasies of power and daydreams of violent social change' which so engaged discontented young men in a politically turbulent decade.[44]Auden's few months in Spain (between January and March 1937) supporting the Republican cause against Franco's right-wing Nationalists brought disillusionment. He was shocked to observe frustrated idealists so readily drawn into bitter factionalism and perpetrating inexcusable violence against the innocent; he was witnessing the worm of self-pity, behind which, he said, 'lies cruelty'.[45]Of greatest abhorrence to him was the sight of despoiled churches in Barcelona and the knowledge that their priests had been murdered. Auden, who admitted that he had consciously ignored and rejected the Church for sixteen years, now realised that its existence and practices 'had all the time been very important'[46] to him. By late 1940, he had returned to the fold as a member of the American Episcopalian church.

Stephen Spender claimed that Auden's emigration to America in 1939 – a move he undertook with Isherwood – was 'an attempt to rediscover his own isolation'[47]after the disheartening political engagement of the 1930s. He knew the role of 'court poet to the Left'[48]to be increasingly a sham, seeing that he had come to believe that poetry had little real influence upon events: 'All the verse I wrote, all the positions I took in the Thirties didn't save a single Jew,'[49]he later acknowledged. The two men were anxious to depart: *Journey to the War* (their account of their visit in 1938 to the Sino-Japanese conflict) was awaiting publication; and the *Oxford Book of Light Verse* (1938), which Auden had edited, was selling well. They arrived in New York in a heavy snowfall on 26th January 1939, the very day on which Barcelona fell to Franco.

By April, Auden had met Chester Kallman, a witty, blond, eighteen-year-old student of Brooklyn Jewish background, who had come to his rented apartment to interview him for a college magazine. Their intimacy, established during a second visit, lasted for the rest of Auden's life, in spite of incompatible sexual preferences and Kallman's roving infidelities. ('On account of you,' he once told Kallman, 'I have been, in intention and almost in act, a murderer.')[50]Kallman, who awakened in Auden a love of opera, was his co-librettist for a number of works, notably Igor Stravinsky's *The Rake's Progress* and Hans Werner

Henze's *The Bassarids*, an adaptation of Euripides' play *The Bacchae*. (Auden also supplied a libretto for Benjamin Britten's *Our Hunting Fathers* – first performed at the Norwich and Norfolk Triennial Festival in 1936 – and for *Paul Bunyan*, his operetta based on the American folk-legend.)

During the 1940s, Auden's poetry began to reflect his reversion to the Christian faith, particularly in works such as *The Double Man* (1941) and *The Age of Anxiety* (1947), his long, Pulitzer Prize poem influenced by his reading of Freud, Marx and Kierkegaard, which explores the condition of loneliness, both universal and private.[51] *Collected Poetry*, an American edition, appeared in 1945 and was revised for publication in England in 1950 as *Collected Shorter Poems*, 1930-1944.

Auden would escape the late spring and summer climate of New York for Europe – from 1948, to the island of Ischia in the Bay of Naples and then (from 1957) to Kirchstetten, a village to the west of Vienna, 'the Karajan city' as he described it, 'where Wagner is played in complete darkness'.[52] In these retreats he could forget about hack-work and the short-term teaching appointments that supplemented his royalties.

In February 1956, he was elected Professor of Poetry at Oxford. 'I'm surprised that the anti-Americans didn't have the political sense to put up a really distinguished scholar, for, if they had, I should immediately have withdrawn',[53] he commented. In addition to delivering the statutory three lectures a year, he was at Christ Church for a month each summer of his five-year tenure, every morning making himself available – in a local café – to undergraduates and others, who met him there for informal literary conversation.[54] When Auden returned from American domicile in 1972, it was to take up permanent residence at Christ Church, in a cottage behind Tom Quadrangle. He had barely a year to live. In one respect, his expectations of Christ Church were disappointed. No longer did the Senior Common Room provide the conviviality he had known as Professor of Poetry when, every night after dinner, there were members in good numbers prepared to stay until a late hour.[55] Increasingly, he kept to the cottage during the day, but would always attend early morning Holy Communion at Christ Church Cathedral on Sunday mornings, a service he appreciated most when Peter Walker, the Suffragan Bishop of Dorchester, was celebrant. 'I can't bear expression being put into the Mass,'[56] Auden remarked. His face now looking utterly 'like a map of physical geography, criss-crossed and river-run and creased with lines' (as Stephen Spender described it in his valediction),[57] Auden would arrive in his carpet-slippers not a minute before the service began and shuffle out just before the close.

With the death of T.S. Eliot in 1965, Auden came to be regarded as English poetry's finest craftsman and a master of poetic mode – 'the urbane, the pastoral, the lyrical, the erudite, the public, and the introspective [that] mingle with great fluency'.[58] Though some of Auden's major later collections, which include *Homage to Clio* (1960), *About the House* (1965) and *City Without Walls* (1969), received mixed reviews, the latter won high praise: the poet Peter Porter, for example, believed it showed Auden's 'nearly flawless knack of getting things right'.[59] And when *The Times* duly published its obituary notice, the headline ran: 'The outstanding English poet of his generation'.

W.H. Auden died of heart failure early on the morning of 29th September 1973. He had declined supper the previous evening and retired to bed, saying he was tired, after giving a poetry-reading to the Austrian Society of Literature in Vienna. He was buried at Kirchstetten on 4th October. As his coffin was being borne from the house, Chester Kallman ordered a pause in the proceedings. 'There is something I have to do,' he said.

Then, in compliance with Auden's wishes, the mourners stood while Siegfried's Funeral March was played on the gramophone.[60]

Loneliness

Gate-crashing ghost, aggressive
invisible visitor,
tactless gooseberry, spoiling
my *tête-à-tête* with myself,
blackmailing brute, behaving
as if the house were your own,
so viciously pursuing
your victim from room to room,
monotonously nagging,
ungenerous jabberer,
dirty devil, befouling
fair fancies, making the mind
a quagmire of disquiet,
weakening my will to work,
shadow without shape or sex,
excluding consolation,
blotting out Nature's beauties,
grey mist between me and God,
pestilent problem that won't
be put on the back-burner,
hard it is to endure you.

Routine is the one technique
I know of that enables
your host to ignore you now:
while typing business letters,
laying the table for one,
gobbling a thoughtless luncheon,
I briefly forget you're there,
but am safe from your haunting
only when soundly asleep.

History counsels patience:
tyrants come, like plagues, but none
can rule the roost for ever.
Indeed, your totter is near,
your days numbered: to-morrow
Chester, my chum, will return.
Then you'll be through: in no time
He'll throw you out neck-and-crop.
We'll merry-make your cadence
with music, feasting and fun.

George Barker 1913 -1991

George Barker's Catholic upbringing instilled in him a sense of sin that was to define his poetic voice. As a youth he would stand staring up at John Henry Newman's statue in the courtyard of the Brompton Oratory, before entering the Oratory House for instruction in the faith. With the traditionalist Father Dale-Roberts, he had read in the *Apologia pro Vita Sua* the passage in which Newman considers the calamity of original sin - one which Barker was to recite throughout his life. 'The human race,' asserts Newman, 'is out of joint with the purposes of its Creator,...a fact as true as the fact of its existence.'[1] This Catholic tenet of human failure was to etch a deep pessimism in Barker[2] and, in the crucible of his later matrimonial infidelities, he would acknowledge the spectre of damnation. His world, wrote his friend the Canadian poet Paul Potts, was 'a long row of confessional boxes where the forgiving priests are his own poems.'[3]

'I am from my mother, Irish,' Barker wrote in his journal. 'Big Mumma' (Marion), a woman of partisan Catholicism from near Drogheda, reigned in the convivial kitchens of the family's various domiciles, where she made the hearts of her guests 'dance and their minds laugh'. Wherever the family lived in London or its suburbs, Barker's father - also George - wished to preserve his own space in living room or snuggery, away from talk of Republican Ireland and, as was needful in London, from all the coming and going of his son's Bohemian set.[4] Unlike his wife, he was of ordered habits. Proud to have served with Kitchener in the Sudan and in the mounted infantry against the Boers, he regarded any suggestion of dilettantism in his son with the utmost suspicion.

When, at the age of nineteen, Barker 'informally seceded' from the faith after 'finding there were seventy women for ten men'[5] amongst the devotees who entered the Oratory, his father, a lapsed Methodist, seemed unconcerned. In the poem that Barker dedicated to his memory - the country churchyard elegy 'At Thurgarton Church' which appeared in *Poems of Places and People* (1971) - he acknowledges the 'unspoken No' of a God dethroned by human indifference, while, as his biographer Robert Fraser puts it, 're-admit[ting] the dialogue of faith by the west door'.[6] Though he had 'forfeited all', the thread of hope is not, perhaps, quite severed; indeed those who await divine wrath may yet encounter, through the mercy of a compassionate God, 'no Judgement Day'.[7]

Thurgarton Church, which Barker first visited in December 1967, soon after moving into Bintry House at Itteringham, lies midway between Aylsham and Cromer. It is a place to which he is known to have returned, mostly alone.

At Thurgarton Church
To the memory of my father

At Thurgarton Church the sun
burns the winter clouds over
the gaunt Danish stone
and thatched reeds that cover
the barest chapel I know.

I could compare it with
the Norse longboats that bore
burning the body forth

in honour from the shore
of great fjords long ago.

The sky is red and cold
overhead, and three small
sturdy trees keep a hold
on the world and the stone wall
that encloses the dead below.

I enter and find I stand
in a great barn, bleak and bare.
Like ice the winter ghosts and
the white walls gleam and flare
and flame as the sun drops low.

And I see, then, that slowly
the December day has gone.
I stand in the silence, not wholly
believing I am alone.
Somehow I cannot go.

Then a small wind rose, and the trees
began to crackle and stir
and I watched the moon by degrees
ascend in the window till her
light cut a wing in the shadow.

I thought: the House of the Dead.
The dead moon inherits it.
And I seem in a sense to have died
as I rise from where I sit
and out into darkness go.

I know as I leave I shall pass
where Thurgarton's dead lie
at those old stones in the grass
under the cold moon's eye.
I see the old bones glow.

No, they do not sleep here
in the long holy night of
the serene soul, but keep here
a dark tenancy and the right of
rising up to go.

Here the owl and soul shriek with
the voice of the dead as they turn
on the polar spit and burn
without hope and seek with
out hope the holy home below.

Yet to them the mole and
mouse bring a wreath and a breath
of the flowering leaves of the soul, and
it is from the Tree of Death
the leaves of life grow.

The rain, the sometime summer
rain on a memory of roses
will fall lightly and come a-
mong them as it erases
summers so long ago.

And the voices of those
once so much loved will flitter
over the nettled rows
of graves, and the holly tree twitter
like friends they used to know.

And not far away the
icy and paralysed stream
has found it also, that day the
flesh became glass and a dream
with no where to go.

Haunting the December
fields their bitter lives
entreat us to remember
the lost spirit that grieves
over these fields like a scarecrow.

That grieves over all it ever
did and all, all not
done, that grieves over
its crosspurposed lot:
to know and not to know.

The masterless dog sits
outside the church door
with dereliction haunting its
heart that hankers for
the hand that loved it so.

Not in a small grave
outside the stone wall
will the love that it gave
ever be returned, not for all
time or tracks in the snow.

More mourned the death of the dog
than our bones ever shall
receive from the hand of god
this bone again, or all
that high hand could bestow.

As I stand by the porch
I believe that no one has heard
here in Thurgarton Church
a single veritable word
save the unspoken No.

The godfathered negative
that responds to our mistaken
incredulous and heartbroken
desire above all to live
as though things were not so.

Desire to live as though the
two-footed clay stood up
proud never to know the
tempests that rage in the cup
under a rainbow.

Desire above all to live
as though the soul was stone,
believing we cannot give
or love since we are alone
and always will be so.

That heartbroken desire
to live as though no light
ever set the seas on fire
and no sun burned at night
or Mercy walked to and fro.

The proud flesh cries: I am not
caught up in the great cloud
of my unknowing. But that
proud flesh had endowed
us with the cloud we know.

To this the unspoken No
of the dead god responds
and then the whirlwinds blow
over all things and beyond
and the dead mop and mow.

And there in the livid dust
and bones of death we search
until we find as we must
outside Thurgarton Church
only wild grasses blow.

I hear the old bone in me cry
and the dying spirit call:
I have forfeited all
and once and for all must die
and this is all that I know.

For now in a wild way we
know that Justice is served
and that we die in the clay we
dread, desired, and deserved,
awaiting no Judgement Day.

Barker became his own man upon the anvil of hardship. '...I never had any Goddamned money,' he admitted in a retrospective documentary made for television in 1987.[8]As a boy in London he recalled searching rubbish bins for scraps and how his mother regularly pawned her wedding ring, something she did to purchase his first type-writer. When Barker dispensed with school at the age of fifteen and became a dedicated autodidact, he never pretended that the gulf of social inferiority could be bridged, or hankered after the clannish complacencies of élitist, literary cliques whose rejection he sensed. In a conversation with Robert Fraser, Sir Stephen Spender admitted that his fellow poet W.H. Auden and their circle had patronised both Barker and Dylan Thomas 'but we were afraid, really, of dirty boots on the carpet.'[9]

When Barker's mentor, T.S. Eliot, recommended he obtain paid employment outside literature in order to mitigate his all-too-frequent pecuniary embarrassment and to avoid the need to blunt his gifts on hack-work, the advice was politely declined. In an essay, 'The Poet as Pariah' (1948), Barker insists instead upon the poet's right to artistic freedom. There is an 'irreconcilable enmity', he says, between the poet and society which 'will never subside, because the day the poet capitulates to society he ceases to be a poet';[10]he feels as did the poet Rainer Maria Rilke, that having a job was 'like death' but without its dignity.[11] It was Eliot who, in the autumn of 1934, persuaded a group of rich friends, among them Lady Ottoline Morrell and Victor Rothschild, to support Barker anonymously. They would make him a quarterly allowance of twenty-five shillings a week for a year.[12]

Subsequently, friends and benefactors eased Barker's financial plight on many occasions throughout his life.

The first of many sojourns in the English countryside began in November 1933 when Barker took his newly-married bride, Jessica (née Woodward), to Worth Matravers on the Isle of Purbeck to keep her two month's of pregnancy from her strict Catholic parents. (Hers was the hymeneal blood, Barker said, that in Richmond Park two years earlier 'first baptised me in Adam's sin.'[13]) It was at Geldeston on the Suffolk-Norfolk border that their daughter Clare was born, and from where Barker made his first visit to Norwich –'a city of memorials and church towers and gardens and large florid public buildings; obscure and angular little alleys with names like Unicorn Way and Swan's Way, Tudor courtyards with fountains dry for years and enormous, meaningless rectangles of shadow and stone where boots or ironmongery or beds are manufactured.'[14] The Castle Museum he described as having 'the appearance of a boy's fort left accidentally on a hill top...'[15]

Of the many cottages Barker rented over the years, mostly in the West Country and in Sussex, a woodman's dwelling on the Petworth Estate, Hearne Cottage, gave him the most treasured seclusion. Here he lived with his lover Betty Cass between 1950 and1957, travelling regularly to London – as was his longtime custom – to talk of poetry with friends and to monitor the progress of books submitted to publishers. This was a fruitful period for Barker which saw the publication of a novel, *Dead Seagull* (1950), with its passages of theological interpretation where he avers that the sin of physical love renders the deity unnecessary.[16] Also in 1950 appeared the first of two books of *The True Confessions of George Barker* whose cynicism, Robert Fraser comments, was 'the lip-service paid by depravity to holiness'.[17] (In a House of Lords debate on 25th November, an enraged Lord Balfour of Inchrye expressed the view that extracts broadcast on the Third Programme compromised the moral integrity of the BBC.[18]) Barker's *True Confessions* was followed by *A Vision of Beasts and Gods* (1954) and his first *Collected Poems* (1930-1955), published in 1957.

The draw of London, even in wartime, was the fraternity of writers and artists who gathered in the pubs of 'Fitzrovia" (to the north of Oxford Street) and Soho, notably the Black Horse (in Rathbone Place) and the Wheatsheaf – and, further afield, the Windsor Castle (in Campden Hill Road). *Habitués* included the artists Robert Colquhoun and Robert MacBride, masters of the conversational gambit of insult,[19] and the poets David Wright and John Heath-Stubbs. As Barker held court in their midst, his talk lunged and parried with hypnotic calculation. In his mid-thirties, among the post-war artistic community at Zennor in Cornwall, Barker's familiar role of 'half spoiled child and half spoiled priest',[20] as Wright later described it, became attuned to that of selfless and assiduous mentor.

In a collection of aphorisms he termed 'Asterisks', Barker surmised that to be happy would necessitate 'the surgical excision of my conscience.'[21] As Elspeth Langlands, his future second wife, discovered on first meeting him in the spring of 1963, Barker could be 'consistently rude and outrageous'[22] until, humbled by his own temperament, he was deeply regretful.[23] (Standing in at short notice for the American poet Theodore Roethke at a writers' conference in Vermont, he caused a group of nuns seated immediately before him to flee the hall by embarrassing them with a wilful outburst of obscenities.[24]) The American novelist Antonia White was much struck by a telling feature of Barker's face, one 'more various than any face I know': his mouth, she observed, could 'be either obstinate, negligible or very sweet and humorous.'[25]

110

When deep in the broil of 'injured love'[26] that so often accompanied his relationship with women, violent temper would burst from the fissures of stress. Changes of mood were exacerbated because Barker took Methedrine and Benzedrine and, from the 1960s, their replacements, 'purple hearts' and 'speed'. On one occasion, the author of a rumour had two teeth broken;[27] on another, a fist blistered one of Cass's eyeballs.[28] Barker admits (in *Dead Seagull*) that sexual desire can be destructive, while believing that 'the cut worm forgives the plough.'[29] In the course of his relationship with the Canadian writer Elizabeth Smart – who re-created it in her fiction *By Grand Central Station I Sat Down and Wept* (1945) – he writes of his wife Jessica 'see[ing] the axe in the air everywhere'.[30] Then, reflecting in his diary upon this protracted betrayal of her, remorse breaks through: 'Virtual assassination of J[essica]. The terrible hell; poor chick!'[31]

At the writing desk, Barker's lodestar was the graft of routine, rather than a waiting upon inspiration. And from younger poets he demanded equal rigour: Heath-Stubbs found him 'a most rigid and ruthless critic of the work of myself and of others'.[32] He eschewed all that was derivative, and sometimes – of a conventional word – he would exclaim (as Ezra Pound had done) 'Make it new!'[33] Barker's own reputation began slipping into its long decline from the mid-1950s onwards, not least because his was a voice which resisted the attempts of academics to classify him as belonging to a 'school' or 'movement'. As early as 1936 W.B. Yeats had commended a new freedom in Barker's handling of traditional metres, pointing out that his verse lacked the 'social passion' and 'sense of suffering' of poets such as MacNeice, Auden and Day-Lewis;[34] and while in the late 1950s his verse was displaying what his detractors saw as 'exhibitionist and rhetorical tendencies', the new generation of poets – Philip Larkin among them – was insisting on what Robert Fraser calls 'the unassuming ordinariness of the speaking voice'.[35]

In this 'middle period', which preceded his move to Norfolk, Barker published (in addition to *A Vision of Beasts and Gods*) the collections *The View from a Blind I* (1962) and *Dreams of a Summer Night* (1966).

Morning in Norfolk

As it has for so long
come wind and all weather
the house glimmers among
the mists of a little
river that splinters, it
seems, a landscape of
winter dreams. In the far
fields stand a few
bare trees decorating
those mists like the fanned
patterns of Georgian
skylights. The home land
of any heart persists
there, suffused with
memories and mists not
quite concealing the
identities and lost
lives of those loved once
but loved most. They haunt it

still. To the watermeadows
that lie by the heart they
return as do flocks of swallows
to the fields they have known
and flickered and flown so
often and so unforgettably over.
What fish
play in the bright wishing
wells of your painted
stretches, O secret
untainted little Bure,
I could easily tell,
for would they not be
those flashing dashers
the sometimes glittering
presentiments, images
and idealizations
of what had to be?
The dawn has brightened the
shallows and shadows and
the Bure sidles and idles
through weed isles and fallen
willows, and under
Itteringham Mill, and
there is a kind of rain-
drenched flittering in the
air, the night swan still
sleeps in her wings and over it all
the dawn heaps up the hanging
fire of the day.

Fowell's tractor blusters
out of its shed and drags
a day's work, like a piled sled
behind it. The crimson
December morning brims over
Norfolk, turning
to burning Turner
this aqueous water colour
idyll that earlier gleamed
so green that it seemed
drowned. What further
sanction, what blessing
can the man of heart intercede for
than the supreme remission
of dawn? For then the mind
looking backward upon its
too sullied yesterday,
that rotting stack of

112

resolution and refuse,
reads in the rainbowed sky
a greater covenant,
the tremendous pronouncement:
the day forgives.

Holy the heart in
its proper occupation
praising and appraising this
godsend, the dawn.
Will you lift up your eyes
my blind spirit and see
such evidence of
forgiveness in the heavens
morning after golden
morning than even
the blind can see?

The move to Bintry House allowed Barker to embrace the role of paterfamilias for so long hampered by the interruptions of temporary homes, his travels and the need to earn a little money from lectureships abroad (in Japan and America). It was a house that brimmed with the children of his unions and their animals and which at weekends was the cherished – and often raucous – centre of conviviality amongst friends.

However 'sullied' Barker felt his yesterdays to have been, the mellow composure of the north Norfolk landscape worked upon him to temper their memory. Driving the children to visit churches, or the beaches of Cromer and Sheringham in summer, he found it 'bare but mysterious',[36] a place which he perceived to possess a 'masculine nobility'.[37] Bintry House itself seemed part of a green idyll, situated as it is near the river Bure and its quivering aspens. Built of Norfolk's familiar red-clay brick as a seventeenth-century farm-house, its rooms were aptly various in meeting the Barkers' eclectic needs; it was a place of crumbling outhouses, stables and a courtyard whose pump was not to survive the impact of a young boy's determined pedalling.[38]

Barker delighted in spinning tales for the children and wrote poems for them too. His three volumes of children's verse were published during these Norfolk years: *Runes and Rhymes and Times and Chimes* (1969), *To Aylsham Fair* (1970) – whose inspiration was the agricultural show held each August Bank Holiday in the park at Blickling Hall – and the bestiary *The Alphabetical Zoo* (1972).

In addition to *Poems of Places and People*, other works of this period included *Dialogues, etc.* (1976), a dark collection that, in part, examines the 'consolatory shade' of death,[39] *Villa Stellar* (1978) – whose final typescript Barker threw into the fire in a moment of inebriate anger – and *Anno Domini* (1983), a poem which Barker said 'operates as if it were a prayer'.[40] *Collected Poems* appeared in 1987.

When Jessica died (in Kentucky) in February 1989, Barker had been unwell for some time with emphysema. Five months later he and Elspeth were married at St Joseph's Roman Catholic church at Sheringham. George Barker died on 27th October 1991 and was buried on the Feast of All Souls in Itteringham churchyard. The legend carved in the granite of the open book that lies at the foot of his grave reads: 'No Compromise'.

NOTES

John Skelton pp.1-11

1. W.C. Hazlitt ed., *Hundred Merry Tales*, 1887, no. xli; quoted in H. L. R. Edwards, *Skelton*, Jonathan Cape, 1949, pp.97-98.
2. Ibid., pp.98-99.
3. William Nelson, *John Skelton, Laureate*, Russell & Russell, New York, 1964, pp.111- 112.
4. E.M. Forster, 'John Skelton', in *Two Cheers for Democracy*, Edward Arnold & Co.,1951, p.145.
5. See J.J. Scarisbrick, *Henry VIII*, Eyre and Spottiswoode, 1968, p.5; also John Bowle, *Henry VIII*, George Allen & Unwin, 1964, p.30.
6. See Arthur F. Kinney, *John Skelton, Priest As Poet*, University of North Carolina Press, 1987, p.88; p.93.
7. The communion-cloth that covers the bread.
8. Purged from her grease.
9. That he would fetch his hounds.
10. Even to the door of the tabernacle, where the body of the Lord is.
11. Why? because the Gospels, holy shells and shell-fish, a hawk and bells and brutish animals, and other such things are all alike to you.
12. E.M. Forster, op.cit., p.146.
13. Psalm 114 v.1: 'I am well pleased [that the Lord hath heard].'
14. Be on his best behaviour.
15. Psalm 129 v.3: 'If [thou shouldest mark] iniquities...'
16. Psalm 129 v.1: 'Out of the depths have I cried [unto thee, O Lord].'
17. 'From the gate of hell...' An antiphon in the Mass for the Dead.
18. Psalm 146 v.1: 'Praise the Lord, O my soul!'
19. 'Grant them eternal rest, O Lord!'
20. Psalm 26 v.13: 'I believe to see the goodness of the Lord.'
21. Psalm 102 v.1: 'Lord, hear my prayer!'
22. 'O God, whose property it is to be merciful and to spare.'
23. J.J. Scarisbrick, op.cit., p.229.
24. William Nelson, op.cit., p.196.
25. T. Tillemans, 'John Skelton, a Conservative', in *English Studies*, 28, p.142; quoted in Stanley Eugene Fish, *John Skelton's Poetry*, Yale University Press, 1965, p.28.
26. Ian Gordon, *John Skelton, Poet Laureate*, Melbourne, 1934, p.69; quoted in Stanley Eugene Fish, ibid., p.28.
27. C.S. Lewis in F. W. Roe ed., *Selections and Essays*, New York, 1918, p.121; quoted in Stanley Eugene Fish, ibid., p.261.

See also

Nan Cooke Carpenter, *John Skelton*, Twayne Publishers Inc., 1967.
Philip Henderson ed., *The Complete Poems of John Skelton*, Dent, 1959 ed.
Maurice Pollet, *John Skelton, Poet of Tudor England*, J. M. Dent, 1971 ed.

Henry Howard, Earl of Surrey pp.12-19

1. W.A. Sessions, *Henry Howard The Poet Earl of Surrey*, Oxford University Press, 1999, pp.338-339.
2. Ibid., p.351.
3. Quoted in Hester W. Chapman, *Two Tudor Portraits*, Jonathan Cape, 1960, p.58.
4. W.A. Sessions, op.cit., p.112.
5. Hester W. Chapman, op.cit., p.50.
6. W.A. Sessions, op.cit., p.362.
7. See J. Huizinga, *The Waning of the Middle Ages*, Penguin ed., 1965, p.55 ff.
8. W.A. Sessions, op.cit., p.207.
9. Lacey Baldwin Smith, *Henry VIII: The Mask of Royalty*, Jonathan Cape, 1971, p.218.
10. W.A. Sessions, op.cit., p.319.
11. Ibid., p.322.
12. Ibid., p.329.
13. Gilbert Burnet, *History of the Reformation*, quoted in Hester W. Chapman, op.cit., p.118.
14. Beverley A. Murphy, *Bastard Prince: Henry VIII's Lost Son*, Sutton Publishing, 2001, pp.120-121.
15. For homoerotic readings of a number of Surrey's texts see Jonathan Crewe, *Trials of Authorship: Anterior Forms and Poetic Reconstructions from Wyatt to Shakespeare*, Berkeley, 1990, pp.48-78; also Jonathan Goldberg, *Sodometries: Renaissance Texts, Modern Sexualities*, Stanford,1992, pp.39-40. and 'Introduction' *Queering the Renaissance*, Durham and London,1994, pp.1-14. These, cited by W.A. Sessions op.cit., p.77 (footnote), have not been consulted by the author.

16. W.A. Sessions, op.cit., p.94.

17. Ibid., p.103.

18. Ibid., p.104.

19. Ibid., p.71.

20. W. J. Courthope, *A History of English Poetry*, 1897, vol. 2, p.185; quoted in W.A. Sessions, op.cit., p.135.

21. See W.A. Sessions, pp.128-135.

22. Hester W. Chapman, op.cit., p.19.

23. Diarmaid MacCulloch, 'Vain, Proud, Foolish Boy:The Earl of Surrey and the Fall of the Howards' in David Starkey ed., *Rivals in Power*, Macmillan, 1990, p.111.

24. W.A. Sessions, op.cit., p.169.

25. Ibid., p.170.

26. Ibid., p.147.

27. Ibid., p.169.

28. Ibid., p.148.

29. Ibid., p.175.

30. See W.A. Sessions, pp.175-176.

31. Ibid., p.177.

32. Ibid., p.261.

33. Introduction to *The Poems of Henry Howard Earl of Surrey*, William Pickering, 1831, p.lxxii.

34. W.A. Sessions, op.cit., p.370.

35. Hester W. Chapman, op.cit., p.115.

36. Lacey Baldwin Smith, op.cit., p.258.

See also

Dennis Keene ed., *Selected Poems*, Carcanet Press, 1985.

Neville Williams, *Henry VIII and his Court*, Weidenfeld and Nicolson, 1971.

Thomas Tusser pp.20-27

1. 1740 ed., p.518.

2. Thomas Tusser, *Five Hundred Points of Good Husbandry* with an introduction by Geoffrey Grigson, Oxford University Press,1984, p.xv.

3. Ibid., p.xv.

4. See Ian Atherton, Eric Fernic, Christopher Harper-Bill and Hassell Smith ed., *Norwich Cathedral: Church, City and Diocese, 1096-1996*, The Hambledon Press, 1996, p.510 ff.

5. George Ewart Evans, *The Farm and the Village*, Faber and Faber, 1969, p.53.

6. Robert Trow-Smith, *English Husbandry From the Earliest Times to the Present Day*, Faber and Faber, 1951, p.86.

7. George Ewart Evans, op.cit., p.53.

8. Robert Trow-Smith, op.cit., p.96.

9. Ibid., p.95.

See also

George Ewart Evans, *Ask the Fellow who Cut the Hay*, Faber and Faber, 1956.

Thomas Fuller, *The History of the Worthies of England*, 1740.

C.S. Lewis, *Oxford History of English Literature*, Oxford University Press, 1954.

John Wood Warter ed., *Southey's Common-Place Book*, Vol. I (1849); Vol. IV (1851).

Robert Greene pp.28-32

1. Nicholas Storojenko, *Robert Greene: His Life and Works, A Critical Investigation*, quoted in Alexander B.Grosart ed., *The Life and Works in Prose and Verse of Robert Greene*, Russell & Russell, 1964, Vol. I, p.8-9.

2. Robert Greene, *All About Cony-Catching*, quoted in Clare Howard, *English Travellers of the Renaissance*, The Bodley Head, 1914, p.55.

3. Ibid., p.54.

4. Thomas Nashe, *Foure Letters Confuted*, quoted in John Clark Jordan, *Robert Greene*, Columbia University Press, 1965 ed., p.2.

5. James Howell, *Letters*; quoted in Clare Howard, op.cit., p.52.

6. Robert Greene, *Quip for an Upstart Courtier*, ibid., p.70.

7. Thomas Hoby, *Travels and Life of Sir Thomas Hoby, Written by Himself*, ibid., p.54.

8. *Dictionary of National Biography*, 1949-50 ed., Vol.VIII, p.513.

9. Ibid., p.510.

10. Ibid., p.513.

11. Alexander B. Grosart ed., op.cit., p.119-120.

12. Robert Greene, *A Notable Discovery of Cozenage*, quoted in Gamini Salgado, *The Elizabethan Underworld*, J.M. Dent,1977, p.32.
13. Ibid., p.33.
14. John Clark Jordan, op.cit., p.191.
15. Ibid., p.200.
16. Quoted in Norman Davies, *The Isles; A History*, Macmillan, pbk. ed. 2000, p.421.
17. John Clark Jordan, op.cit., p.4.
See also
Robert Bell ed., *The Poems of Robert Greene, Christopher Marlowe and Ben Jonson*, George Bell and Sons (Bohn's Standard Library Edition), 1878.

John Taylor pp.33-37

1. Cited in Bernard Capp, *The World of John Taylor, the Water Poet 1578-1653*, Oxford University Press, 1994, p.65.
2. Ibid., p.87.
3. Ibid., p.53.
4. Ibid., p.51.
5. Ibid., p.54.
6. Ibid., p.54.
7. Ibid., p.54.
8. Ibid., p.78.
9. *Dictionary of National Biography*, Vol.XIX, 1963-64 ed., p.432.

Richard Corbett pp.38-41

1. Oliver Lawson Dick ed., *Aubrey's Brief Lives*, Secker & Warburg, 1958 ed., p.72.
2. See J.E.V. Crofts, *A Life of Bishop Corbett 1582-1635*, in E.K. Chambers ed., *Essays and Studies of The English Association*, Oxford University Press, 1924, Vol.X, pp.76-77.
3. H.R. Trevor-Roper, *Archbishop Laud 1573-1645*, Macmillan, (2nd Ed.) 1962, p.196.
4. Ibid., p.196.
5. Charles Carlton, *Archbishop William Laud*, Routledge & Kegan Paul, 1987, p.105.
6. H.R. Trevor-Roper, op.cit., p.196.
7. J.A.W. Bennett and H. R. Trevor-Roper, *The Poems of Richard Corbett*, Oxford University Press, 1955, p. xix.
8. Ibid., p.63.
9. Ibid., p.xxii.
10. Cited in Oliver Lawson Dick, op.cit., p.73.
11. Charles Carlton, op.cit., p.87.
12. Fuller, *Worthies* (1662), sig. L.II2., quoted in J. A. W. Bennett and H. R. Trevor-Roper op.cit., p.xxxv.
13. William John Charles Moens, *The Walloons and their Church at Norwich 1565-1832*, Lymington, 1888, p.22.
14. J.E.V. Crofts, op.cit., p.88.
15. Quoted in J.E.V. Crofts, ibid., p.95.
16. Ibid., p.72.
17. Oliver Lawson Dick ed., op.cit., p.72.
18. See *To The Lord Mordant upon his returne from the North*, ll.132-134, in J.A.W. Bennett and H.R. Trevor-Roper, op.cit., p.28.
19. Ibid., p.xiv.
20. *Dictionary of National Biography*, 1963-64 ed., Vol.IV, p.1129.
21. J.A.W. Bennett and H. R. Trevor-Roper, op.cit., pp. xli-xlii.
See also
Charles Carlton, *Charles I, The Personal Monarch*, Routledge & Kegan Paul, 1995 ed.
Samuel Smiles, *The Huguenots, Their Settlements, Churches and Industries in England and Wales*, John Murray, 1880.

Thomas Shadwell pp.42-47

1. Albert S. Borgman, *Thomas Shadwell: His Life and Comedies*, Benjamin Blom, New York, 1969, p.12.
2. Montagu Summers ed., *The Complete Works of Thomas Shadwell*, The Fortune Press, 1927, Vol. II, p.280.
3. *Works of Mr. Thomas Brown*, 1720, Vol.II, p.165; quoted in Albert S. Borgman, op.cit., p.12.
4. Quoted in Albert S. Borgman, op.cit., p.9; p.10.
5. Montagu Summers ed., op.cit., Vol.I, p.xxvii.

6. Kenneth Hopkins, *The Poets Laureate*, The Bodley Head, 1954, p.33.
7. See John Spurr, *England in the 1670s: 'This Masquerading Age'*, Blackwell, 2000, p.165 ff.
8. Quoted in Albert S. Borgman, op.cit., p.50.
9. Quoted in Michael W. Alssid, *Thomas Shadwell*, Twayne Publishers, 1967, p.22.
10. William Meyers, *Dryden*, Hutchinson, 1973, p.73; *MacFlecknoe*, l.103.
11. Preface to *The Humorists*, Montagu Summers ed., op.cit., Vol.I, p.184; p.183.
12. Michael W. Alssid, op.cit., p.24.
13. Quoted in Michael W. Alssid, p.23.
14. Preface to *The Sullen Lovers*, Montagu Summers ed., op.cit., Vol.I, p.11.
15. Ibid., p.lxxii.
16. Epilogue to *The Humorists*, Vol.I, ll.15-18.
17. R. Latham and W. Matthews ed., *The Diary of Samuel Pepys*, Vol. IV, p.181; quoted in John Spurr, op.cit., p.110.
18. John Spurr, ibid., p.112.
19. Aphra Behn, *Oroonoko, The Rover and Other Works*, Penguin, 1992, p.174; quoted in John Spurr, op.cit., p.3.
20. Ibid., p.106.
21. *Coffee Houses Vindicated*, 1675, p.1; quoted in John Spurr, op.cit., p.104.
22. Montagu Summers ed., op.cit.,Vol.I, p.181.
23. Ibid., p.182.
24. Ibid., Vol.III, p.19.
25. Ibid., Vol.II, p.102.
26. Ibid., Vol.V, p.99; p.100.
27. Ibid., p.251; p.248.
28. Ibid., Vol.III, p.283.
29. Kenneth Hopkins, op.cit., p.40.
30. Quoted in Kenneth Hopkins, ibid., p.41.
31. *Gentleman's Journal*, January 1691/2; quoted in Albert S. Borgman, op.cit., p.84.
32. See Michael W. Alssid, op.cit., p.116.

William Cowper pp. 48-56

1. Josiah Bull, 'The Early Years of the Poet Cowper at Olney', *The Sunday at Home, A Family Magazine*, 1866; quoted in Maurice J. Quinlan, *William Cowper, A Critical Life*, University of Minnesota Press, 1953, p.86.
2. 'Lines Written Under the Influence of Delirium'; *Cowper Poetry and Prose* selected by Brian Spiller, Rupert Hart-Davis, 1968, p.54.
3. David Cecil, *The Stricken Deer or The Life of Cowper*, Constable, 1947 ed., p.29.
4. David Newsome, 'Newman and the Oxford Movement' in *The Victorian Crisis of Faith*, Anthony Symondson ed., SPCK, 1970, p.87.
5. David Cecil, op.cit., p.127.
6. Ibid., p.79.
7. Ibid., p.94.
8. 'Looking Upward in a Storm', Brian Spiller, op.cit., p.156.
9. Line 2 of the first 'Divine Meditation'; James King, *William Cowper*, Duke University Press,1986, p.85.
10. Cowper to the Revd. William Unwin, 26th September 1781, Brian Spiller, op.cit., p.637.
11. 'Temptation', Brian Spiller, op.cit., p.155.
12. 'The Progress of Error', ibid., p.221.
13. James King, op.cit., pp.144-145,152.
14. Cowper to Anne Bodham, 27th February 1790; Mary Barham Johnson, unpublished 'Letters & Diaries of the Norfolk Families, Donne & Johnson, 1766-1917', Vol.I, 1987, p.50.
15. James King, op.cit., pp.186-187.
16. Cowper to Harriot Hesketh, 26th January, 1790; quoted in James King, p.186.
17. Cowper had the added responsibility, in the absence of their sick incumbent, for the two nearby parishes of Yaxham with Welborne (whose advowsons he had put himself into debt to purchase).
18. Mary Barham Johnson, op.cit., p.89.
19. Ibid., p.99.
20. Ibid., p.89.
21. 'The Shrubbery, Written in a Time of Affliction', Brian Spiller, op.cit., p.55.
22. Ed. 1798, Bk. I, ch.8; Brian Spiller, ibid., p.138.

Thomas Hood pp. 57-64

1. *The Times*, 27th October, 1843. Quoted in John Clubbe, *Victorian Forerunner: The Later Career of Thomas Hood*, Duke University Press, 1968, p.152.
2. J.C. Reid, *Thomas Hood*, Routledge & Kegan Paul, 1963, p.7.
3. David Newsome, *The Victorian World Picture*, John Murray, 1997, p.23.
4. Quoted in J.C. Reid, op.cit., p.238.
5. Ibid., p.7.
6. John Heath-Stubbs, *The Darkling Plain: A Study of the Later Fortunes of Romanticism in English Poetry from George Darley to W.B. Yeats,* Eyre & Spottiswode, 1950, p.54.
7. Lloyd N. Jeffrey, *Thomas Hood*, Twayne Publishers, 1972, p.81.
See also
Laurence Brander, *Thomas Hood*, Longmans, Green & Co., 1963.
Poems of Thomas Hood, Oxford University Press 'The World's Classics' ed., 1907.

George Borrow p.65-76

1. A. Egmont Hake, 'Recollections of George Borrow', *The Athenaeum*, 2807 (13 August 1881), 209; quoted in Michael Collie, *George Borrow Eccentric*, Cambridge University Press, 1982, p.3.
2. David Williams, *A World of His Own: The Double Life of George Borrow*, Oxford University Press, 1982, p.7.
3. Michael Collie, op.cit., p.235.
4. See Clement King Shorter, *George Borrow and His Circle*, Hodder and Stoughton, 1913, p.120 ff.; also James Hooper, *Souvenir of the George Borrow Celebration*, Jarrold & Sons, 1913, pp.23-24.
5. David Williams, op.cit., p.11.
6. Michael Collie, op.cit., p.21.
7. Ibid., p.23.
8. David Williams, op.cit., p.18.
9. Michael Collie, op.cit., p.25.
10. Clement King Shorter, op.cit., p.109.
11. Ibid., p.111.
12. James Hooper, op.cit., p.25.
13. Quoted in Michael Collie, op.cit., p.230.
14. John Murray, *Good Words*, quoted in Michael Collie, p.231.
15. Frederick Toates, *Obsessional Thoughts and Behaviour*, Thorsons,1990, p.165.
16. See *Lavengro*, Ch. xxxix.
17. *Literary Gazette*, 16th July 1825; quoted in Shorter, op.cit., p.106.
18. Darlow, *Letters of George Borrow to the British and Foreign Bible Society*, p.4.; quoted in Michael Collie, p.64.
19. W.I. Knapp, *Life, Writings and Correspondence of George Borrow*, Vol.I, pp.313-14; quoted in Michael Collie, p.147.
20. Michael Collie, op.cit., p.140.
21. Betty Miller ed., *Elizabeth Barrett to Miss Mitford*, 1954, p.182; quoted in Robert R. Meyers, *George Borrow*, Twayne Publishers Inc., 1966, p.63.
22. *Quarterly Review* (March 1843), p.171; quoted in Robert R. Meyers, op.cit., p.62.
23. Robert R. Meyers, op.cit., p.63.
24. Ibid., p.62.
25. *Encyclopaedia Britannica*, Eleventh Edition, Vols.III-IV, p.275; quoted in Robert R. Meyers, op.cit., p.62.
26. Michael Collie, op.cit., p.199.
27. *Wild Wales* (Collins); quoted in Michael Collie, op.cit., p.240.
28. See Frederick Toates, op.cit., p.165.
29. David Williams, op.cit., p.162.
30. *Eastern Daily Press*, 30th September 1913.
See also
William A. Duff, *George Borrow in East Anglia*, David Dutt, 1896.
Gillian Fenwick ed., *Proceedings of the 1993 George Borrow Conference*, The George Borrow Society, 1994.
Richard Ford, Leslie Stephen and George Saintsbury, *Borrow Selections with Essays*, Oxford University Press, 1924.
Clement Shorter ed., *The Works of George Borrow*, Norwich Edition, John Constable, 1923.

Algernon Charles Swinburne pp.77-86

1. Quoted in Rikky Rooksby, *A.C. Swinburne: A Poet's Life*, Scolar Press, 1997, p.8.
2. *Selections from Byron;* quoted in Rikky Rooksby, op.cit., p.128.
3. *Lesbia Brandon;* quoted in Rikky Rooksby, p.7.
4. Cecil Y. Lang ed., *The Swinburne Letters*, Yale University Press, 1959-62, Vol.1, p.303; quoted in Jean Overton Fuller, *Swinburne: A Critical Life*, Chatto & Windus, 1968, p.172.
5. Quoted in Rikky Rooksby, op.cit., p.212.
6. James Douglas, *Theodore Watts-Dunton: Poet; Novelist; Critic*, Hodder and Stoughton, 1904, p.106.
7. Theodore Watts, *Alwyn;* quoted in James Douglas, p.342.
8. Cecil Y. Lang ed., op.cit., Vol.5, p.37.
9. Clement William Scott, *Referee* (April 18,1909), p.13; quoted in Cecil Y. Lang ed., op.cit., Vol.5., p.37n.
10. David Newsome, *The Victorian World Picture*, John Murray,1997, p.248; Donald Thomas, *Swinburne: The Poet in his World*, Weidenfeld and Nicolson, 1979, p.111.
11. Bonamy Dobree ed., *Swinburne. Poems*, Penguin, 1961; quoted in A.N. Wilson, *God's Funeral*, John Murray, 1999, p.216.
12. Harold Nicolson, *Swinburne*, 1926, p.43; quoted in Donald Thomas, op.cit., p.36.
13. Edmund Gosse, *The Life of Algernon Charles Swinburne*, 1917, p.41; quoted in Donald Thomas, ibid., p.36.
14. Cecil Y. Lang ed., op.cit., Vol.1, p.236n; quoted in Rikky Rooksby, op.cit., p.149.
15. Donald Thomas, op.cit., p.39; p.40.
16. See David Newsome, op.cit., p.185.
17. Edmund Gosse, op.cit., p.324; quoted in Donald Thomas, p.50.
18. John A. Cassidy, *Algernon C. Swinburne*, Twayne Publications, 1964, p.46.
19. Quoted in Rikky Rooksby, op.cit., p.216.
20. John A. Cassidy, op.cit., p.122.
21. Quoted in Rikky Rooksby, op.cit., p.217.
22. Bernard M.G. Reardon, *Religious Thought in the Nineteenth Century*, Cambridge University Press, 1966, p.197; John A. Cassidy, op.cit., p.121.
23. Jean Overton Fuller, op.cit., p.158.
24. Rikky Rooksby, op.cit., p.186.
25. Edmund Gosse, op.cit., p.290; quoted in Rikky Rooksby, p.19.
26. Edmund Gosse,op.cit., pp.24-5; quoted in Rikky Rooksby, p.9.
27. Edmund Gosse,op.cit., p.319; quoted in Donald Thomas, op.cit., p.22.
28. Lionel James, *A Forgotten Genius: Sewell of St Columba's and Radley*, Faber, 1945, pp.228-9; quoted in Rikky Rooksby, op.cit., p.33.
29. Edmund Gosse, op.cit., p.292; quoted in Rikky Rooksby, p.33.
30. Edmund Gosse, p.26; quoted in Donald Thomas, op.cit., p.26.
31. Rikky Rooksby, op.cit., p.37; quoted by permission of the Provost and Fellows of Worcester College, Oxford.
32. Donald Thomas, op.cit., p.93.
33. Georges Lafourcade, *Swinburne: A Literary Biography*, 1932; cited in Rikky Rooksby, op.cit., p.77.
34. John A. Cassidy, op.cit., p.71.
35. Edmund Gosse, op.cit., pp. 95-6; quoted in Donald Thomas, op.cit., p.92.
36. Rikky Rooksby, op.cit., p.198.
37. C.L. Cline ed., *Letters of George Meredith*, 1970, Vol. I, p.106; quoted in Donald Thomas, op.cit., p.73.
38. Rikky Rooksby, op.cit., p.138.
39. Ibid. p.138
40. Derek Hudson, *Munby: Man of Two Worlds*, 1972; see Donald Thomas, op.cit. p.138.
41. Oswald Doughty, *Dante Gabriel Rossetti*, 1949, p.323; see John A. Cassidy, op.cit., p.65.
42. John A. Cassidy, p.132.
43. Cecil Y. Lang ed., op.cit., Vol.4, p.139n; quoted in Rikky Rooksby, p.276.
44. Donald Thomas, op.cit., pp.204-5.
45. Edmund Gosse, *Swinburne. An Essay Written in 1875*, 1925; quoted in Rikky Rooksby, op.cit., p.102.
46. W.H. Mallock, *Memoirs of Life and Literature*, 1920; quoted in Rikky Rooksby, p.102.
47. Rikky Rooksby, op.cit., p.267.
48. James Douglas, op.cit., p.270.
See also
The Poems of Algernon Charles Swinburne, 6 Vols., Chatto & Windus, 1904.

R. H. Mottram pp.87-95

1. R.H. Mottram, *The Window Seat or Life Observed*, Hutchinson, 1954, p.45.
2. Ibid., p.43.
3. Ibid., p.45.

4. Ibid., p.43.
5. Ibid., p.86.
6. Ibid., p.34.
7. Ibid., p.28.
8. Ibid., p.50.
9. Ibid., p.21.
10. R.H. Mottram, *Vanities and Verities*, Hutchinson, 1958, p.115.
11. Ibid., p.115.
12. Ibid., p.114.
13. R.H. Mottram, *The Window Seat or Life Observed*, op.cit., p.76.
14. Ibid., p.76.
15. Ibid., p.53.
16. Ibid., p.64.
17. Ibid., p.69.
18. Ibid., p.72.
19. Ibid., p.92.
20. Ibid., p.145.
21. Ibid., p.217.
22. See *The Window Seat or Life Observed*, chapter xxxii, pp.221 ff.
23. Ibid., p.226.
24. Ibid., p.161.
25. R.H. Mottram, *Another Window Seat or Life Observed*, Hutchinson, 1957, p.71.
26. Ibid., p.50.
27. Ibid., p.45.
28. Ibid., p.57.
29. *Vanities and Verities*, p.45.
30. *Another Window Seat or Life Observed*, p.58.
31. Ibid., p.62.
32. Ibid., p.59.
33. *Vanities and Verities*, p.175.
34. *The Window Seat or Life Observed*, pp.88-89.
35. Ibid., p.90.
36. Ibid., p.90.
37. *Another Window Seat or Life Observed*, p.153.
38. Ibid., p.155.
39. Ibid., p.74.
40. *The Window Seat or Life Observed*, p.160.
41. Ibid., p.160.
See also
R.H. Mottram, *The Twentieth Century: A Personal Record*, Hutchinson, 1969.

W.H. Auden pp.96-104

1. 'Letter to Lord Byron'; see Edward Mendelson, ed., *The English Auden: Poems, Essays and Dramatic Writings 1927-1939*, Faber and Faber, 1977, p.192.
2. Stephen Spender, 'W. H. Auden and His Poetry' in Monroe K. Spears, *Auden: A Collection of Critical Essays*, Prentice Hall, 1964, p.36.
3. Edward Mendelson, ed., op.cit., p.46.
4. Humphrey Carpenter, *W.H. Auden: A Biography*, George Allen & Unwin, 1981, p.14.
5. 'The Prophets' in Edward Mendelson ed., *W. H. Auden: Collected Poems*, Faber and Faber, 1976, p.203.
6. *Southern Review*, Summer 1940, p.78; quoted in Humphrey Carpenter, op.cit., p.14.
7. Humphrey Carpenter, op.cit., p.13.
8. Richard Davenport-Hines, *Auden*, Heinemann, 1995, p.23.
9. Ibid., p.23.
10. Christopher Isherwood, *Lions and Shadows: an education in the twenties*, Hogarth Press, 1938, p.181f; quoted in Humphrey Carpenter, op.cit., p.21.
11. Quoted in Humphrey Carpenter, ibid., p.40.
12. Quoted in Humphrey Carpenter, ibid., p.37.
13. Edward Mendelson ed., *The English Auden*, op.cit., p.322.
14. Quoted in Humphrey Carpenter, op.cit., p.28.
15. *The Dyer's Hand*, Faber and Faber, 1963, p.36; quoted in Humphrey Carpenter, ibid., p.34.

16. W. H. Auden, 'A Literary Transference', *Southern Review*, 6 (1940), p.78-9; quoted in Richard Davenport-Hines, op.cit., p.42.
17. Edward Mendelson ed., *The English Auden*, op.cit., p.325.
18. Steve Benson (with Martin Crossley Evans), *I Will Plant Me a Tree: An Illustrated History of Gresham's School*, James and James, 2002, p.37.
19. Edward Mendelson ed., *The English Auden*, p.323.
20. Ibid., p.323.
21. Robert Medley in Stephen Spender ed., *W. H. Auden: A Tribute*, Weidenfeld and Nicolson, 1974, p.38.
22. Edward Mendelson ed., *The English Auden*, op.cit., p.323.
23. Richard Davenport-Hines, op.cit., p.40.
24. Edward Mendelson ed., op.cit., p.324.
25. Robert Medley, op.cit., p.39.
26. Ibid., p.40.
27. Quoted in Humphrey Carpenter, op.cit., p.40.
28. Ibid., p.41.
29. W. H. Auden, *Forewords and Afterwords*, Faber and Faber, 1973, p.509; quoted in Humphrey Carpenter, op.cit., p.37.
30. Quoted in Humphrey Carpenter, ibid., p.364.
31. Quoted in Richard Davenport-Hines, op.cit., p.56.
32. Ibid., p.56.
33. Stephen Spender, *World Within World*, Hamish Hamilton, 1951, p.54.
34. Ibid., p.55.
35. Humphrey Carpenter, op.cit., p.68.
36. P.H. Salus and P.B. Taylor, *For W.H. Auden*, February 21, 1972, Random House, 1972, p.49; quoted in Humphrey Carpenter, op.cit., p.305.
37. Humphrey Carpenter, ibid.., p.45.
38. Unpublished memoir of Auden by V.M. Allom; quoted in Humphrey Carpenter, ibid., p.81.
39. Thom Gunn, *Shelf Life*, 1994, p.178; quoted in Richard Davenport-Hines, op.cit., pp.54-55.
40. Humphrey Carpenter, op.cit., p.112.
41. *Forewords and Afterwords*, p.69f; see Humphrey Carpenter, ibid., pp.160-161.
42. Humphrey Carpenter, ibid., p.113.
43. 'Mr Auden's Poetry', *Adelphi*, December 1930, p.251f; quoted in Humphrey Carpenter, ibid., p.117.
44. G. S. Fraser, 'The Career of W.H. Auden' in Monroe K. Spears ed., op.cit., p.84.
45. W.H. Auden, 'The Heresy of Our Time', *Renascence*, 1 (Spring 1949), p.24; quoted in Richard Davenport-Hines, op.cit., 168.
46. W.H. Auden, essay in James Pike, *Modern Canterbury Pilgrims*, 1956, p.41; quoted in Richard Davenport-Hines, op.cit., p.169.
47. Stephen Spender in Monroe K. Spears ed., op.cit. p.35.
48. Edward Mendelson ed., *The English Auden*, op.cit., p.xix.
49. Peter Parker ed., *The Reader's Companion to Twentieth Century Writers*, Fourth Estate, 1995, p.35
50. Verse-letter to Chester Kallman, Christmas Day, 1941; quoted in Humphrey Carpenter, op.cit., p.311.
51. Humphrey Carpenter, ibid., p.332.
52. W.H. Auden, 'Going into Europe', *Encounter*, 20 (January 1963), p.54; quoted in Richard Davenport-Hines, op.cit., p.297.
53. Joanna Richardson, *Enid Starkie*, Oxford University Press, 1973, p.198; quoted in Humphrey Carpenter, p.382.
54. Humphrey Carpenter, ibid., p.384.
55. Ibid., p.444.
56. *Theology*, November 1977, p.430; quoted in Humphrey Carpenter, ibid., p.446.
57. Stephen Spender ed. and 'Valediction', *W.H. Auden: A Tribute*, op.cit., p.245.
58. Margaret Drabble ed., *The Oxford Companion to English Literature*, Oxford University Press, 1998 ed., p.49.
59. Peter Porter, 'Faber and Faber Limited', *London Magazine*, 9 (October 1969), p.421; quoted in Humphrey Carpenter, op.cit., p.332.
60. Humphrey Carpenter, ibid., p.452.
See also
W.H. Auden, *Collected Poems* (Edward Mendelson ed.), Faber & Faber, 1976.
Charles Osborne, *W.H. Auden: The Life of a Poet*, Harcourt Brace Jovanovich, 1979.

George Barker pp. 105-113

1. John Henry Newman, *Apologia pro Vita Sua*, Ch.V; quoted in Robert Fraser, *The Chameleon Poet: A Life of George Barker*, Jonathan Cape, 2001, p.17.

2. Patrick Swift, 'Prolegomenon to George Barker', in John Heath-Stubbs and Martin Green ed., *Homage to George Barker on his Sixtieth Birthday*, Martin Brian & O'Keeffe, 1973, p.60.
3. Paul Potts, 'Many Happy Returns', in John Heath-Stubbs and Martin Green ed., ibid., p.11.
4. Robert Fraser, op.cit., p.8.
5. George Barker, *Essays*, MacGibbon & Kee, 1970, p.72.
6. Robert Fraser, op.cit., p.420.
7. Ibid., p.421.
8. Ibid., p.xi.
9. Ibid., p.46.
10. George Barker, op.cit., p.122.
11. Ibid., p.120.
12. Robert Fraser, op.cit., p.73.
13. Quoted in Robert Fraser, ibid., p.33.
14. Ibid., pp.65-66.
15. Ibid., p.99.
16. Ibid., p.295; see Martha Fodaski, *George Barker*, Twayne Publishers, 1969, p.121.
17. Robert Fraser, op.cit., p.267.
18. Ibid., p.317.
19. Ibid., p.234.
20. Quoted in Robert Fraser, ibid., p.272.
21. George Barker, op.cit., p.135.
22. Quoted in Robert Fraser, op,cit., p.379.
23. Ibid., p.313.
24. Ibid., p.354.
25. See Robert Fraser, ibid., p.87; and book cover.
26. Elizabeth Smart, *By Grand Central Station I Sat Down and Wept*, 1945, p.97; quoted in Robert Fraser, op.cit., p.177.
27. Robert Fraser,ibid., p.183.
28. Ibid., p.313.
29. Quoted in Robert Fraser, ibid., p.296.
30. Ibid., p.172.
31. Ibid., p.157.
32. John Heath-Stubbs, *Hindsights: An Autobiography*, Hodder & Stoughton, 1993, p.151; quoted in Robert Fraser, op.cit., p.277.
33. Robert Fraser, ibid., p.277.
34. W.B. Yeats ed., *The Oxford Book of Modern Verse*, 1892-1935, Oxford University Press, p.xli; quoted in Robert Fraser, op. cit., p.80.
35. Robert Fraser, ibid., p.328 & 329.
36. Ibid., p.416.
37. 'The oak and the olive', l.42.
38. Robert Fraser, op.cit., p.451.
39. 'To John Berryman', l.73.
40. Robert Fraser, op.cit., p.483.
See also
George Barker, *Collected Poems*, edited by Robert Fraser, Faber & Faber, 1987.